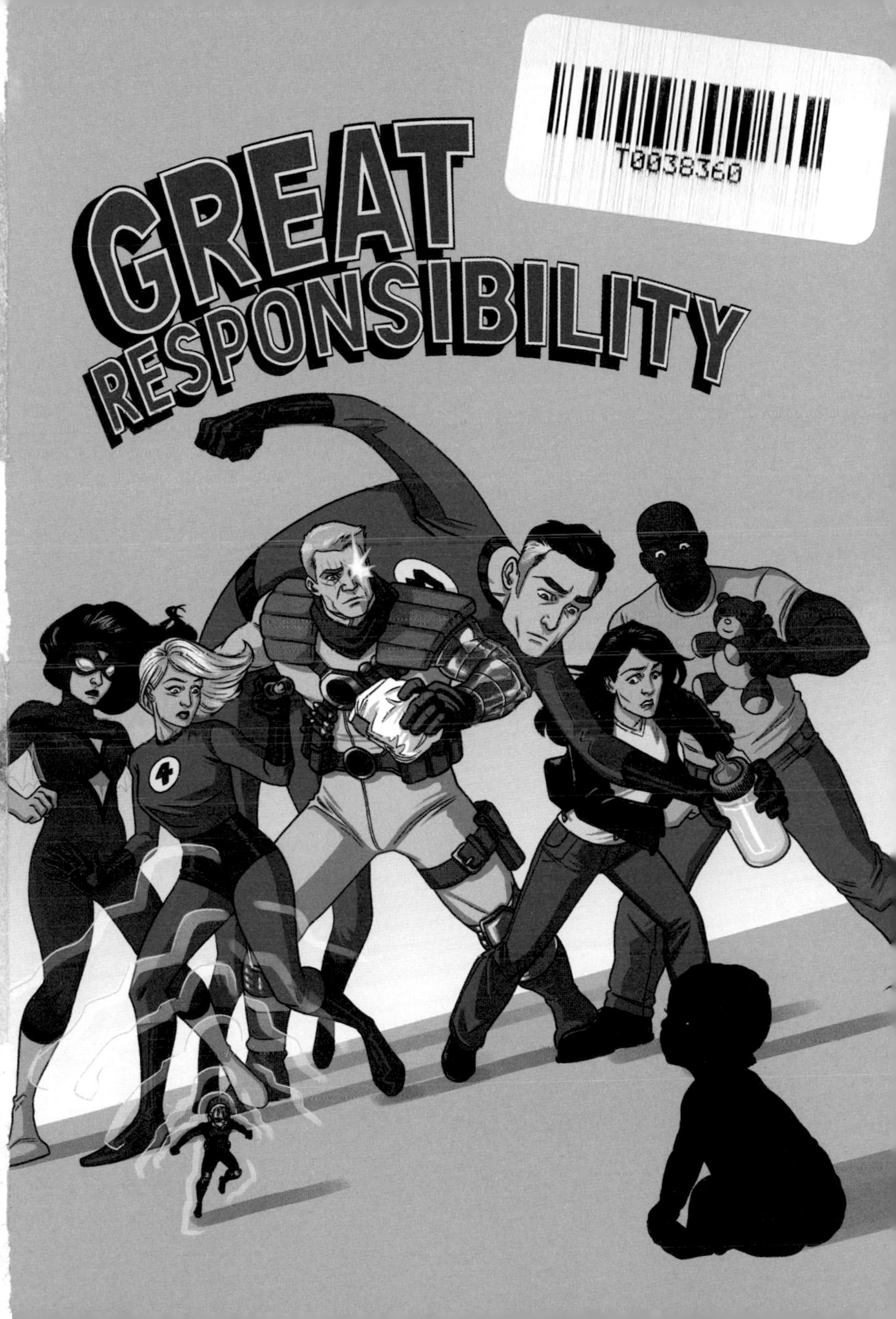
GREAT
RESPONSIBILITY

MARVEL

A PARENTING GUIDE WITH A SUPER-HEROIC TWIST!

GREAT RESPONSIBILITY

RAISING YOUR LITTLE HERO FROM TODDLER TO TEEN

JENN FUJIKAWA and TROY BENJAMIN

SMART POP

Smart Pop Books
An Imprint of BenBella Books, Inc.
Dallas, TX

Smart Pop is an imprint of BenBella Books, Inc.
10440 N. Central Expressway Suite 800
Dallas, TX 75231
smartpopbooks.com | benbellabooks.com
Send feedback to feedback@benbellabooks.com

BenBella and *Smart Pop* are federally registered trademarks.

Printed in the United States of America
10 9 8 7 6 5 4 3 2 1

Library of Congress Cataloging-in-Publication Data is available upon request.
ISBN 9781637743522 (print)
ISBN 9781637743539 (ebook)

Editing by Elizabeth Smith
Copyediting by Michael Fedison
Proofreading by Sarah Vostok
Text design and composition by Tara Long
Cover design by Brigid Pearson
Cover illustration by Megan Levens
Cover lettering by J.K. Woodward
Printed by Versa Press

MARVEL PUBLISHING
Jeff Youngquist, VP, Production and Special Projects
Sarah Singer, Editor, Special Projects
Jeremy West, Manager, Licensed Publishing
Sven Larsen, VP, Licensed Publishing
David Gabriel, SVP Print, Sales & Marketing
C.B. Cebulski, Editor in Chief

TO THE MEGAVERSE COSMIC ENTITIES

TYLER AND MASON,
MY HOPE IS THAT YOU WILL ALWAYS
WORK TOGETHER TO BUILD A BETTER UNIVERSE.

—J.F.

FOR MY SUPER PARENTS

JIM AND ISABELL.
AND FOR HAZEL AND FELIX,
FOR A CRACK AT BEING ONE TOO.

—T.B.

CONTENTS

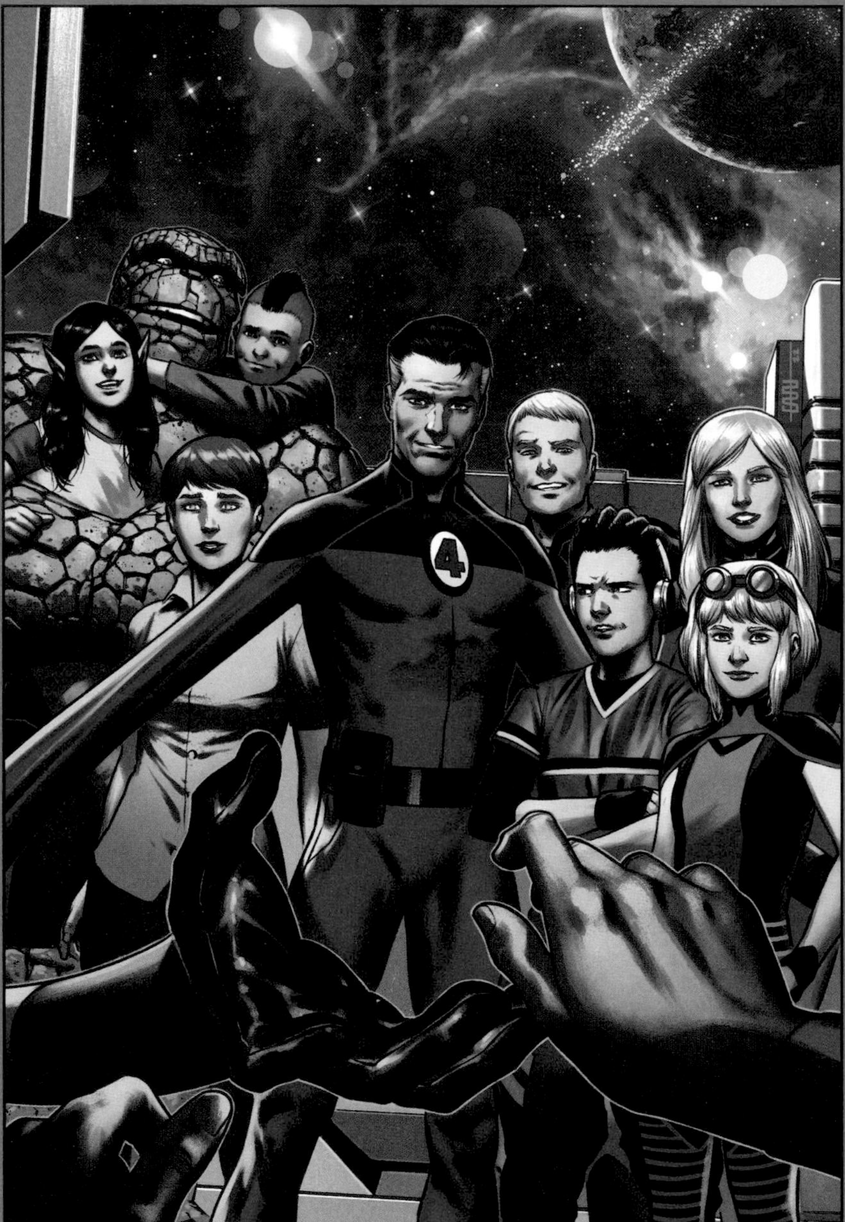

INTRODUCTION

GREETINGS, TRUE BELIEVERS AND PARENTS ACROSS THE UNIVERSE AND BEYOND! Welcome to the astonishing universe of being responsible for a living, breathing creature, while also being a Marvel fan. Parenthood is difficult and challenging, but a whole lot of fun too. And while this process doesn't come with a manual, *Great Responsibility: Raising Your Little Hero from Toddler to Teen* is the closest you'll find to a field guide for the true believer embarking upon the greatest Journey into Mystery of all: parenthood.

If you're looking for expert information that will give you all the answers, or profound advice that will always steer you in the right direction, well, this isn't it. Truth is, that book of wisdom may not exist. Don't expect this to be a magical tome filled with enchantments to cast bedtime sleep spells on your children. And, while there's not a "Doctor" title in front of our names (though we've been known to yell "DOOM!" while hiding in our Latverian sanctuaries for no reason), we are two authors who are also parents doing our best, raising our kids to the best of our abilities and hoping that the Eye of the Watcher will show us the way. Parenting is an experience that's inherently unique to each and every person. Being a parent is hard, and though Marvel characters have telepathic powers and inhuman abilities, they still have the same hurdles and frustrations as everyday parents. They just have to combat invading Kree warriors while doing it. See, you're already one step ahead!

The good news is that, as a Marvel Comics fan, you've already been exposed to some of the most valuable wisdom to apply to your life as a parent. From expectant parents to those ready to release their Gifted Youngsters out into the Sentinel-filled world, we look toward the most beloved Marvel characters to glean wisdom and inspiration, all with a sense of humor to help navigate the most daunting tasks of parenting.

Familial relationships within Marvel have incredible themes that are often mirrored in our everyday lives. Whether it's the struggles of raising a God of Thunder and a God of Mischief concurrently, or dealing with your angsty teen's mutant tendencies, much can be learned through our favorite characters' journeys. Let's face it, turning your kids into well-rounded humans (who don't scheme to collect Infinity Gems for world domination) can be just as hard as getting gamma radiation out of a baby's onesie. Hopefully with this book by your side, both will be a little easier.

Structured chronologically to parallel a child's development from newborn to young adult, we'll explore themes, challenges, lessons, pitfalls, tips and tricks, and advice all with the trademark Marvel wit, wisdom, and earnestness that is sure to bring tears of both laughter and emotion. Think of this as your Book of Vishanti... with possible paths to enlightenment. This book may not solve all your parenting problems, but it will make raising your little super hero a lot more fun.

—JENN AND TROY

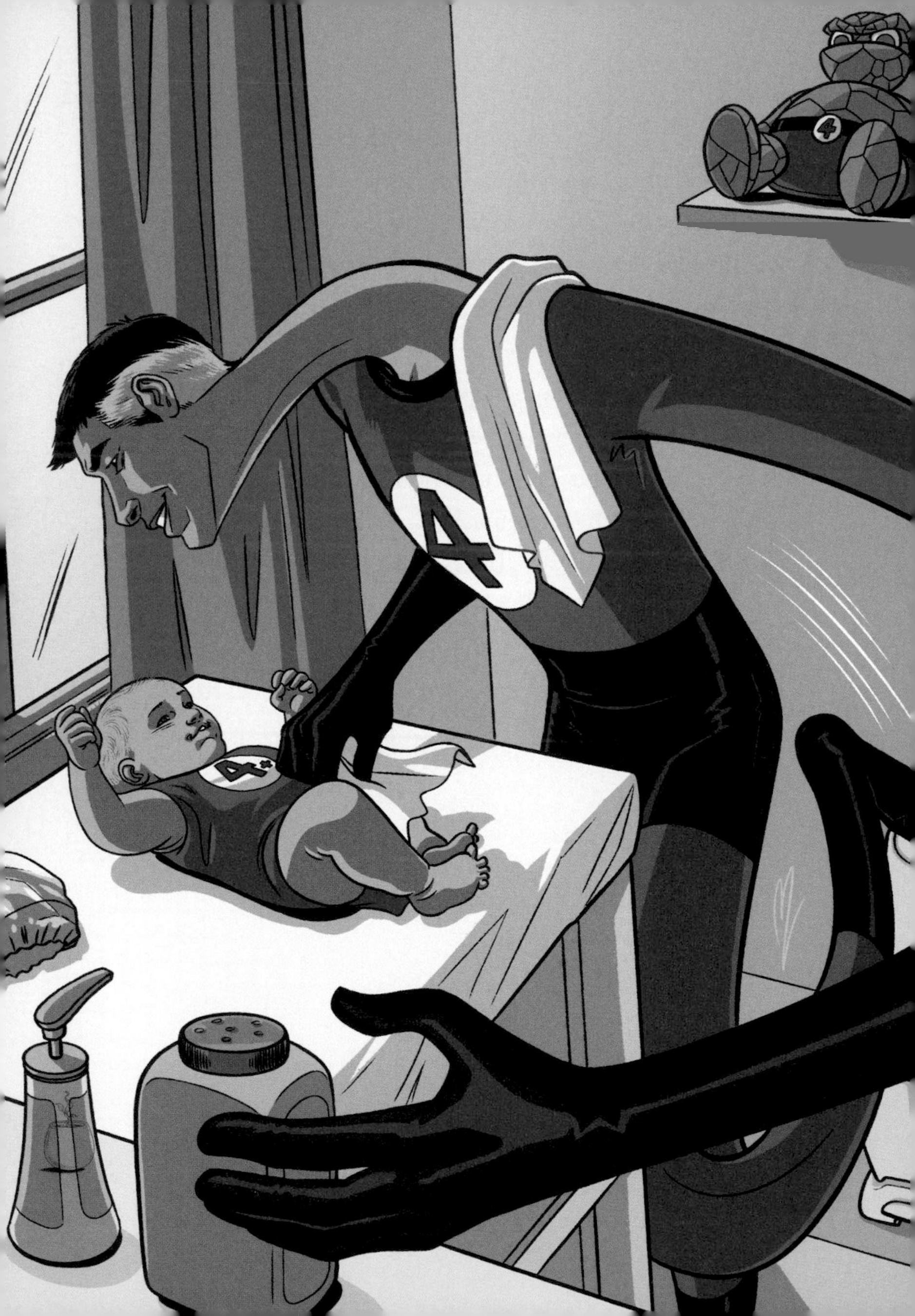

CHAPTER 1

IT'S A TERRAN!

BABIES AND TODDLERS: AGES 0 THROUGH 3

SO YOU'RE EXPECTING A BABY? Congratulations! Becoming a parent can be one of the most rewarding experiences of your life. Successfully raising a small Terran from a Throg-sized nugget to a strong and independent young adult will make you feel like you could take on the whole Kree empire. Heck, you could even do it with one hand tied behind your back. Undoubtedly, since receiving the news you'll be a parent soon, there have to be a million things running through your head. But you've got this. Even if you're double-agenting between S.H.I.E.L.D. and Hydra while simultaneously moonlighting as an Avenger like Jessica Drew, you'll still somehow manage to find the time to be an amazing and present parent.

If it's your first time having a child, don't worry. That lump you feel in the bottom of your stomach is normal. Unless you ate something funky, in which case it's probably a bad Clowntown burger. Either way, that feeling will pass in time. That sensation may infrequently return, but it can be used as fuel for the courage and confidence you'll need for the next few decades. Seriously, if it was the burger and it keeps happening, maybe try something else on the menu next time?

Let's start with the daunting stuff. To put it bluntly, the world you used to know is over. Is that a sharp corner? The baby will want to bonk their head on it. Will intergalactic forces zealously want to utilize your child to open a wormhole for invading forces? Possibly. You're going to be on high alert twenty-four hours a day, seven days a week. You have to put yourself in Cable's shoes and look at your new baby as Hope Summers: the last of mutantkind. Everything and everyone has it out for them, including themselves. It is your sworn duty to protect them at all costs. Not to mention, you'll be doing it all on empty because you yourself haven't slept since the new addition entered our realm. You're going to need stamina, patience, and probably a whole lot of caffeine. But hey, caffeine has been shown to extend your life span. Bonus!

WAY OUT
IS UP
PAGES 10-11
SAVAGE LAND
SHOCKER!
DAILY GLOBE
MORTGAGE!
ER OUR SWEEPSTAKES! DETAILS, PAGE 38
SERVING NEW YORK AND THE WORLD
LY GLOBE EXCLUSIV
AVENGERS
BABY BO
PAGES 4-5
THE PROUD PARENTS
AN REVEAL

If this is your second kid (or beyond), luckily you already have an inkling of the future that lies ahead. This precognitive ability is a lot like Ruth Aldine / Blindfold's extraordinary talents and can be a valuable asset as a parent. You won't exactly have the ability to predict a civil war between factions of the X-Men. But you will be equipped with the knowledge to expect when you will—and when you won't—be able to sleep for the next several years, what cues mean hunger or tiredness, and how to efficiently and properly extinguish an incendiary outburst of flames. But don't be fooled. Second kids are always different. All the telepathic mind tricks you used on the first one may not work the second time around.

Waiting for a newborn's arrival can be overwhelming. The uncertainty feels like an unstoppable Wakandan maglev train speeding into a foggy horizon. The fog is thick with nerves associated with everything from driving to the hospital to the next eighteen years. As you head into the fog, you realize parenting carries the weight of great sacrifice. If you're like Jessica Drew / Spider-Woman, pregnancy means cutting out your favorite foods. But it also means being infuriatingly sidelined and sitting out field missions and having to call the shots from the van, watching as someone else does a job you know you could do in your sleep. Or also like

Jessica, suddenly and confusingly wondering if your prized motorcycle is an acceptable and safe mode of transportation during the pregnancy.

Jessica Drew made a conscious decision to become a parent, with the understanding it would change her life immeasurably. But even going into it with that knowledge, she didn't realize the massive pendulum shift that she'd have to combat. She could no longer run headfirst into danger feeling like she had nothing to lose. With a dependent being as your charge (especially a newborn that will try to fling itself into an interdimensional portal multiple times daily and it's your job to stop that), your priorities are about to make a massive metamorphosis right down to the DNA. Ultimately, the transformation will be worth it. Every time that little one smiles at you, the first time they giggle at your antics, and the first time they telekinetically raise a building block to top off a tower, you'll feel it down to your very core.

Suggested Reading

Dennis Hopeless and Javier Rodriguez's run on Spider-Woman from 2015 should be essential reading to any Marvel fan who is expecting a newborn. In fact, both creators had newborns themselves at the time they were crafting Jessica Drew becoming a parent.

CHOOSING A BABY NAME THE MARVEL WAY

The first parenting task to tackle is awarding your tiny flesh-being a name that they'll have for the rest of eternity. Jessica Jones and Luke Cage referred to their newborn baby as "You-To-Be-Named" for far too long before landing on Dani's moniker. Luckily, one can look to the Marvel stable of characters to instill their hopes, dreams, and aspirations of what attributes and personality quirks they desire their child to have.

Here are some options to consider. Try them out by saying the names out loud for a few weeks, then switch it up to see how it feels. With a little trial and error, you'll develop a sense for those you prefer. And hopefully, you and your child won't be stuck with a name like Negasonic Teenage Warhead and a world full of regret.

TIP We suggest you treat the names you're considering for your baby with S.H.I.E.L.D.-like confidentiality. Even if you consider telling one trusted friend, loose lips sink Helicarriers. You'll find that friends' and family's opinions of names will introduce bias to your decision-making.

CLASSIFIED

ALISON—If you wish stardom and the life of a pop superstar for your daughter, consider naming her after Alison "Dazzler" Blaire.

AMADEUS—If you wish your child to become the ultimate combo of Brawn and brains, naming them after Amadeus Cho is a smashing way to go.

BRUCE—If you hope for your child a genius-level intelligence and selfless courage to always do what's right, naming them after the Incredible Hulk is wise. And, even if they're a physicist like Dr. Bruce Banner, as long as you keep them away from gamma radiation, everything should be fine.

BUCKY—The name of Winter Soldier and onetime Captain America James Buchanan Barnes is perfect for parents who wish to instill strength and loyalty in their son.

CAROL—Whether she takes the prefix of Ms. or Captain, give your daughter the strength to go higher, farther, and faster by naming her after Carol Danvers. She may even let you call her by the nickname "Cheeseburger."

CINDY—She may find discomfort with crowds, but naming your daughter after Cindy Moon / Silk guarantees she'll have a kind and generous heart.

CLINT—Giving your son Clinton "Clint" Barton's—A.K.A. Hawkeye's —name guarantees a sharpshooter with a sense of adventure.

DOREEN—Your daughter has the potential to be a hero as a young teenager. She'll also have a plethora of furry rodent friends that she can chat up at the local park if you name her after Doreen "Squirrel Girl" Green.

ELEKTRA—Give your daughter a name that instills resilience and an honorable soul, but keep her away from mystical ninja cults.

EMIL—You may not want association with the criminally leaning and destructive Abomination. But a strong name like Emil should protect your kid with the thick skin they'll need for life.

EMMA—Diamonds are her best friend, and possibly her greatest shield against attack. Mix that with a penchant for taking charge, teaching the next generation, and getting the best of Wolverine, with Emma Frost's name.

FELICIA—Naming your daughter after a world-famous Black Cat burglar is a bold choice. But Felicia's leadership capabilities and the slipperiness that helps her get out of a bind with ease are admirable traits.

HANK—If you want to bestow upon your child the mind of a genius and a mane of hair requiring habitual conditioning, consider giving them the Beast's name in honor of Henry "Hank" McCoy.

HOPE—If you think highly enough of your daughter to believe she's the last savior of mutantkind, and if you trust a time-traveling soldier to babysit from time to time, name her after Hope Summers.

JEAN—Bonus points if you can work "Grey" in as a middle name. Do everything in your power to keep her away from the Phoenix Force, just to be safe.

JUBILATION—You would rarely call your daughter by her full name and opt instead to call her Jubilee on the regular. And the namesake would match her jubilant personality.

KATHERINE "KITTY"—She'll be your pride and joy. But if she has Kitty Pryde's ability to phase through walls, then sending her to her room and making sure she stays there may prove futile.

LEMAR—Give your son the strength of ten, and a fighting chance against a horde of zombies when the apocalypse comes, with the name of Battlestar, Lemar Hoskins.

LOGAN—Nothing says making sure they bounce right back from potential injury like naming them after Weapon-X, adamantium-outfitted Wolverine. But beware of their short temper.

LUKE—The Power Man himself, Luke Cage will assure the strength of your son's body and mind, and that he'll be a leader among the community.

MONICA—Your daughter will have limitless energy if you name her after Photon—Monica Rambeau. She'll also be good in a fight should vampires ever take over the French Quarter.

NATASHA (or consider Natalia as an alternative)—Your daughter will have a killer instinct, the mind of the greatest tactician, and the agility of a high-flying acrobat if you name her after the Black Widow herself.

MATT—Want to make sure that your son has no fear? Give him the name of the Daredevil himself, Matt Murdock.

ODIN—It'll be tough to keep your son humble if their namesake is the immortal ruler of Asgard. But the All-Father is also powerful and wise.

ONYEKA—Give your daughter the strength of ten Dora Milaje warriors, and the name to match.

ORORO—If your daughter is born during the storm of a century, and you have an inkling that the storm may be of her creation, Ororo might be the perfect name. The regal name may also open a door to be queen of Wakanda someday.

OTTO—Gift your son a keen mind and ability to multitask as if they have six arms, by naming them after Doctor Octopus, Otto Octavius.

PHIL—Give your son the top cheese and assure they'll be as loyal, trustworthy, and kid-at-heart as everyone's favorite S.H.I.E.L.D. agent, Phil Coulson.

PIOTR—Stronghold your son from the harsh realities of the world and name him after Colossus. Just remember, impenetrable armor can't stop a broken heart.

RAVEN—With Mystique's name, your daughter will always find a way to blend into a crowd, literally and figuratively. She may also find herself drawn to those with magnetic personalities.

REED—No matter what dimension, the name Reed Richards is a beacon toward the smartest person in the room. Bonus points that it will give your son flexibility and versatility too.

REMY—Naming your child after the charming and cunning Gambit assures your son will have endless energy and a knack for super-charging objects with the touch of a finger.

ROBBIE—Want to give your child a fiery personality? Naming him after Robbie Reyes, the latest in a long line of Ghost Riders, is a surefire win.

SAM—Give your kid the ability to soar to the highest heights and possibly take over the mantle of Captain America from Steve Rogers, by naming him after Sam Wilson.

SCOTT—If you want your son to be technically engineering–minded, consider naming him after Scott Lang, the second Ant-Man.

SHARON—Are you a descendant of a S.H.I.E.L.D. legend? Does the number 13 not carry the unlucky stigma for you and your daughter? Both should be telltale signs your daughter should share a name with Peggy Carter's niece.

SHURI—She'll always be the smartest person in the room, as well as the most technologically savvy, and she probably won't be upset by having to help you troubleshoot issues with your personal devices.

STEPHEN—If you're the type of parent encouraging your child to be a doctor at every turn, why not name them after world–class surgeon and Sorcerer Supreme, Doctor Stephen Strange?

STEVE—"Steve" may take flack for being a generic and overused name. But if you name your son after the Star-Spangled Man, Steve Rogers, you're giving them a name that carries strength of heart, conviction, resilience, determination, and the ability to sleep soundly for decades.

SUSAN (or just Sue)—Naming your daughter after the Invisible Woman might make you fear that she sometimes won't be seen, but she'll find strength within herself to counter the possible introverted tendencies.

TONY—Your son could have a keen intellect for engineering, a savvy business sense, and the infinite charm and wit of the most notable playboy philanthropists by being named after Tony Stark.

VALKYRIE (or Brunhilde, if you're courageous)—Your daughter will carry souls to Valhalla and have the strength to face Durok the Demolisher head-on.

WADE—You can gift your son with a quickness of tongue, ability to heal wounds instantly, and a never-ending hunger for chimichangas by giving him Deadpool's common namesake.

WANDA—Every day with your daughter will be magic. There may occasionally be the accidental incendiary fire, love affairs with the ruler of Atlantis and a cybernetic Avenger, and refuge after the House of M.

THE IMPORTANCE OF PLANNING

Any hero worth their salt knows everything starts with a plan. And a backup plan for when that one fails. Then a second backup plan for when Galactus unexpectedly appears to devour your home planet. For good measure, you'll also want an escape plan when those all go sideways.

When you're expecting, the best favor you can do for yourself is to have plans. That's right, plural. All the plans. Not just a "birth plan." Those are for mere mortals. You should be prepared for *anything*. Getting to the hospital, retreating off-world, temporal incursion, furnishing the baby's room, setting up a neural link blockage shield, where/when/how to change diapers at home comfortably... All the plans. Why? The more that you've planned out, the more your brain can focus on the chaotic unexpected. There is a certain Murphy's Law to parenthood. Anything that could go wrong will. Even if you've mapped out twelve routes to the hospital, you haven't foreseen a Skrull invasion of the hospital. Okay, so the Skrulls may not infiltrate your local maternity ward, but you may need to deal with an invasion of unwanted in-laws. Which in some ways could be a lot worse. If you've explored how to deal with the sit-

uations you can at least premeditate, you'll have more brainpower for the Skrulls. Wait... Unless your in-laws are *also* Skrulls. That sounds messy. Honestly, we're not sure how to help you there.

Initiate a conversation with yourself using the following inner-dialogue prompts. Fill in the blanks to these prompts with as many potential things you can creatively think of, then answer those questions for yourself. Make sure to write down all of your answers. The second thing you'll quickly realize as a parent is that stress and sleeplessness greatly affects your memory. The first thing, we humble authors cannot recall. Writing things down for the rest of your life is key. (And yes, that was a dad joke. Those will also just start naturally happening and there's nothing we can do about it.)

WHAT STEPS DO I NEED TO TAKE TO _____?

Examples: make sure the new baby is insured, notify Damage Control in the event of catastrophic property damage, etc.

HOW WOULD I REACT IF _____?

Examples: our doctor is out of town when labor begins, Sentinels suddenly tear the roof off the hospital, etc.

WHAT WILL I NEED IN THE EVENT THAT _____ HAPPENS?

Examples: more hospital stay than a day or two is needed, a time incursion sends us all a hundred years into the future during birth, etc.

WHAT IF I'M OUT AND THE BABY _____?

Examples: drops a number two so explosive it wrecks their clothes, etc.

This exercise will help you organically premeditate the unexpected. Creative brainstorming and preplanning is half of parenting. What if I'm out and the baby blows out a diaper...twice? What if cosmic radiation is present in the mother and she needs to be transported to the Negative Zone to save both her and the baby? What steps do I need to take to get the baby into the car when they come home from the hospital? How would I react if the baby is born and a time traveler appears with a cautionary prophecy? What will I need in the event that A.I.M. knocks the power out while we're in the hospital during labor? And from that, it'll help you start creating lists and plans. The more you do that, the less overwhelmed you'll feel.

As you start to explore these scenarios, you'll soon realize you'll need to have a Natasha Romanoff–like go bag at the ready. Don't call it a diaper bag. That's demeaning toward the importance of the tools and utilities contained within. This carryall will be used at the hospital and for first outings to the park, that rare lunch with your friends who are dying to see your newborn, and even for interdimensional travel. So make sure that it's something sturdy, versatile, and you're not totally embarrassed with it strapped to your back. You'll always be prepared with your go bag by your side.

THINGS TO HAVE IN YOUR GO-BAG

(WHETHER FOR THE BABY BIRTH OR FOR AN OFF-WORLD AVENGERS EMERGENCY)

1. At least two days' worth of clean clothing for you and your partner

2. Outfit for the baby. Something warm, something that controls electricity or absorbs solar flares. Don't forget gloves and a blanket

3. Toothbrush and toothpaste

4. Negative Zone Cosmic Radiation Control Rod

5. Deodorant (trust us)

6. Glasses (or an extra pair of contacts) – if needed

7. Phone charger

8. Camera (even if there's one on your phone)

9. Bluetooth speaker for tunes

10. Mandalay Gem (to give everyone an extra energy boost)

AVENGERS, ASSEMBLE!
(TO TAKE CARE OF THIS BABY)

Knowing when and how to ask for help is an eternal struggle for new parents. Having a solid support system to rely upon is crucial. To put things in perspective, the seemingly invincible Jessica Jones and Luke Cage had to assemble the Avengers during the birth of their daughter, Danielle. In Jessica Jones' case, she had a hospital staff that turned her away, claiming inadequate facilities to deliver a genetically enhanced mother's child. An emergency airlift and escort to the Sanctum Sanctorum was necessary. *(Very specific circumstances. When labor starts, you shouldn't need a Quinjet to take you to Doctor Strange to deliver your baby.)* However, amassing your own Personal Avengers to assemble when you most need them can be indispensable. The reassurance that one phone call or group text can lend you a sympathetic ear of a fellow parent, a good friend, or a wise mentor can be the difference between calm and

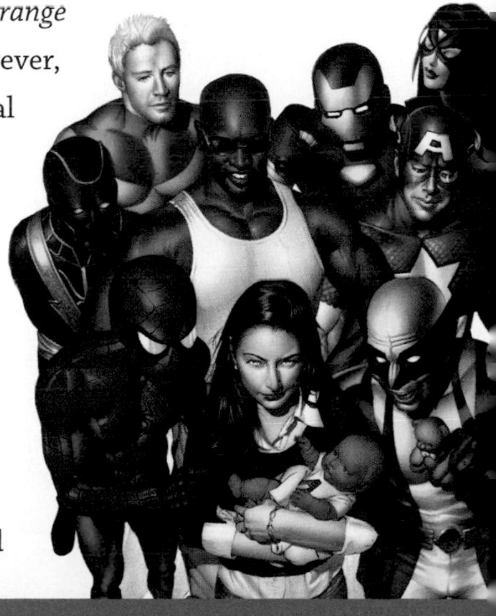

chaos. You can really only talk to yourself so much before people start to question your stability.

Your Personal Avengers are especially important during the first three months of parenthood, which are the equivalent of an endurance test in the Danger Room. As Jessica Drew says while having brunch with her fellow Spider-Women at Earth-65's Clowntown, being a parent is "pretty amazing when it's not totally exhausting and overwhelming." Jessica quickly learned that newborns require undivided attention 24/7.

THINGS TO REMEMBER TO GET YOU THROUGH THE FIRST THREE MONTHS OF HAVING A BABY:

1. It's only three months. Tony Stark has taken longer vacations.

2. Sometimes the baby will scream and cry when you've tried everything and they're not hungry, tired, or need to be changed. And that's okay.

3. But sometimes that Hulk rage is only because they need to fart.

4. Actually, a lot of the common issues are gastrointestinal.

And when their needs aren't met, they sonically screech like Angar the Screamer. She needed a lifeline for a five-minute adult conversation to save her sanity and called upon her Spider-friends for a day out. If you don't have the luxury of a dimensional travel watch to skip

TIP Don't forget: even those with enhanced abilities need to take leave. And that goes for maternity/paternity leave or just setting the baby down in the crib and taking five minutes to breathe. Lean on your Personal Avengers for help.

to another Multiverse for brunch with your besties, you still have to find your own ways to at least give yourself a few moments.

Shortly after the birth of their daughter, Jessica Jones and Luke Cage are faced with a tough dilemma: either they sign the Superhuman Registration Act and receive the pay and benefits of a government job, or live a life on the run as fugitives. It's a difficult decision. They feel a responsibility both as heroes—with a community that looks up to them—and as parents who need to consider the well-being of their daughter. Ultimately, Jessica flees with the baby to Toronto and Luke stays behind to join Captain America in what becomes a civil war among heroes. While you may not necessarily be faced with a similar decision to flee with your child or face an army of Stark-tech-enhanced S.H.I.E.L.D.

agents knocking at your door, the responsibility of taking care of your child can often require sacrifices. Like taking a job with better pay and benefits, even though it doesn't necessarily follow your dreams. Or turning your spare room into a bedroom for the new arrival. Sometimes even the smallest of these sacrifices in the name of your new child can be heroic.

TIP

Remember the two-hour rule! For the first three months of the baby's life, you'll most likely be doing something every two hours: feeding, napping, or changing a diaper. Use those times in between to make like Makkari and move at the speed of light to accomplish as much as you can.

WEATHERING TANTRUM STORMS

Eventually, your child is going to find their voice—for better or worse. As strong opinions are formed, and the ability to vocalize those opinions manifests, so begin the mood swings and tantrums. There will be explosive and irrational outbursts of emotion that will have you convinced your child has absorbed the Phoenix Force and is hell-bent on the world burning. Tantrums are a fact of life. Frankly, a lot of the biggest Marvel events have occurred because one or more characters were throwing epic tantrums. From age one until adulthood (unfortunately), your child will become and remain a symbiote that feeds off negative vibes and manifests them into their own reciprocal energy. How we choose to harness and deal with those tantrums is instilled within us at an early age.

Take the mutant appropriately named Tantrum as an example. He channels the fear and anger of those around him and turns it into rage-filled power that allows him to smash through buildings and go toe-to-toe with the Incredible Hulk. Your child could just as easily take their tantrum-filled rage and accomplish similar feats, with similarly measured property damage. Arming them with the ability to take four deep breaths, count to four, and calm themselves can go a long way. You'll also find that if you kick your own anger and rage up to eleven, they'll harness that energy just like Tantrum and reciprocate it right in your face. It's good to keep your cool and show them that you can control your anger too.

Note: This is all totally different when they become teenagers. Their tantrums come with logical rebuttals, louder and more articulate voices, and far more strength. For a preview of that Skaar, son of Hulk–like fun, skip ahead to the "Teens: Ages 13 Through 18" chapter.

Throughout this book, you'll often see the importance of open communication as the key to so many developmental stages. You may *think* you are communicating effectively, but at different stages of your child's life, their communication powers are still maturing and there may be a disconnect. Use these charts throughout your kid's life cycle to understand where their strengths and weaknesses lie.

COMMUNICATION POWER GRID – AGES 0 TO 3

Awareness:	████████████████████
Verbalization:	⟋⟋⟋⟋⟋⟋⟋⟋
Comprehension:	███⟋⟋⟋⟋⟋
Combativeness:	███⟋⟋⟋⟋⟋

SURVIVING SLEEP DEPRIVATION
AND THE LIGHT AT THE END OF THE BIFROST

The first year of your child's life, your sleep totals will certainly suffer. Be prepared for nights where you only get two or three combined hours of actual sleep. Gradually, getting consecutive hours of sleep will once again return to your daily routine. In fact, generally once you're past the first year, you're in the clear. You can use that milestone as light at the end of your sleepy tunnel—it will get better. And here's the best part: Sleep returning to your daily routine is also timed to a pretty fun window from ages one through three, where you'll really get to know your kid.

You've heard about the "terrible twos," but don't let them scare you off. While it's not exactly a walk through Central Park, age two predominantly is wonderful. This is when your kid is developing their sense of humor and their imagination, and everything is entertaining to them no matter how trivial you may find the subject. They'll say funny things you'll remember for the rest of their lives. They're strange little Doop-like characters who one moment seem to possess the intellect of a genius, and the next minute they'll be babbling in their own gibberish language as they cram breakfast cereal into the Quinjet's air vents. Sure, there are tantrums and lapses from time to time, but those are few and far between. They're fun little gremlins by age two. But it goes by fast. Enjoy it and make sure to live in the moment while it lasts.

Age three, on the other hand, is one to look out for. While the "terrible twos" may be overexaggerated, the "threenager" phase is no joke. Just like every hero with an origin story, the next chapter of life is going to test every bit of the strength and stamina that you've built up since their birth and poke holes at any potential weaknesses.

TIP

Between spit-ups, blowouts, or the occasional exposure to cosmic radiation, keeping a newborn's clothing clean, or at least visibly clean, can be a heroic effort all its own. Getting gamma radiation (or worse) out of a baby onesie can be an impossible feat. If regular washes and spot treatments aren't doing the trick, and a decontamination chamber wasn't on your baby registry, sometimes you'll just have to let certain clothes go. Throw them in the hazardous biocontaminant bin and forget about them. Or be prepared to let those stains ride as little weathered badges to intimidate potential baby foes.

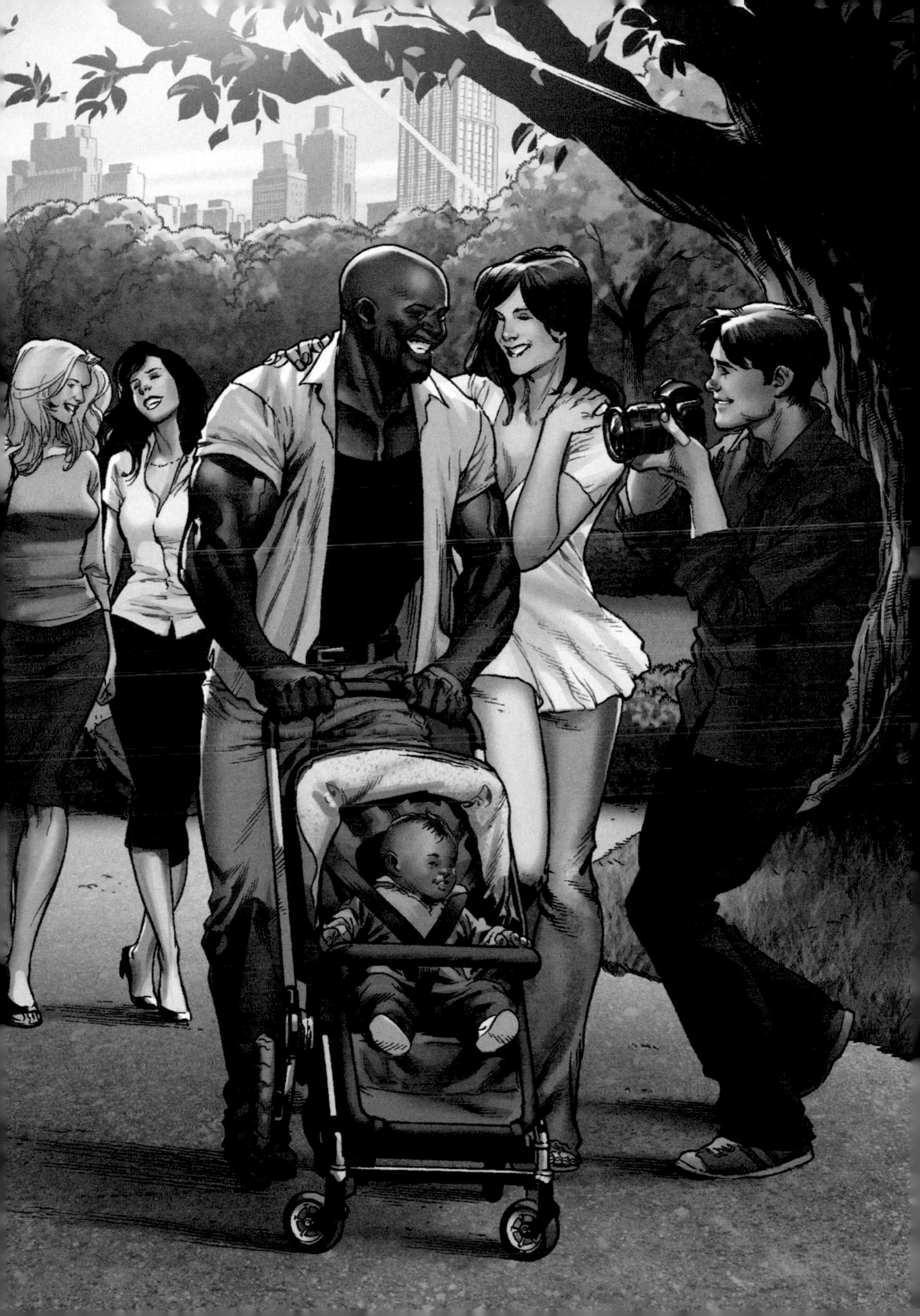

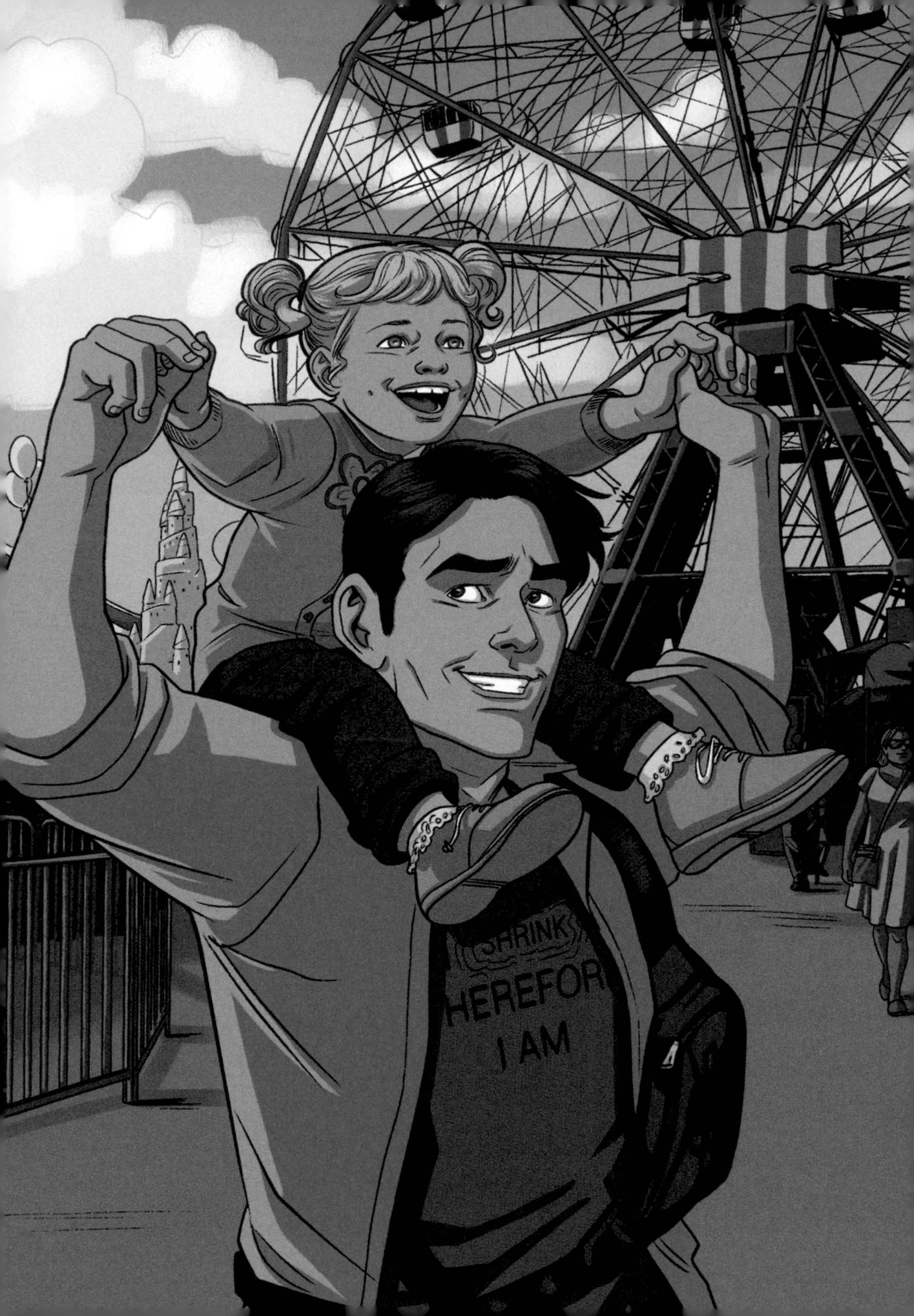
SHRINK
HEREFOR
I AM

CHAPTER 2

EVEN A WORLD-EATER CAN BE PICKY

PRESCHOOLERS: AGES 3 THROUGH 5

THE FIRST FEW YEARS OF PARENTHOOD WERE ABOUT SURVIVAL—both for you and for them. You didn't magically concoct twins from the ether as Wanda Maximoff did with Billy and Tommy, so the experience of having a newborn was probably equal parts magical and exhausting. Now you get into real hands-on parenting. In these next few years, experiences, words of advice, emotions, and behaviors are imprinting upon them and molding them into the human they'll be for the rest of their lives. Here is where you really have to prove your mettle.

The pressure of knowing these experiences and behaviors are such important building blocks in your child's development can sometimes inhibit a quick reaction or decision just when they're needed. It can also leave you second-guessing yourself. Get ready to question if the stern way you just told your child not to color on the wall with crayon has given them a complex. The fact of the matter is, you haven't trained for this. Aside from reading books of sage-like wisdom (thanks for this purchase, by the way), you'll also be experiencing a lot of these moments for the first time too. As a wise man once said, you need a license to drive or fish, but they'll let anyone be a parent. Keep that in mind when feelings of inadequacy creep into your thoughts.

Hop into the Spider-Copter with us for a moment, and take a look at things from a ten-thousand-foot view. Parenting is structured quite a bit like the natural storytelling arcs of a monthly comic book. The journey of a hero mirrors much of what is happening to you as a parent. Take Spider-Man for example.

In the first full year of *The Amazing Spider-Man*, in 1963, Peter Parker is still getting a sense of his powers and learning to walk before he can web-sling. It's his origin story and early adventures, filled with self-discovery. Likewise, in the first year as a parent, you met

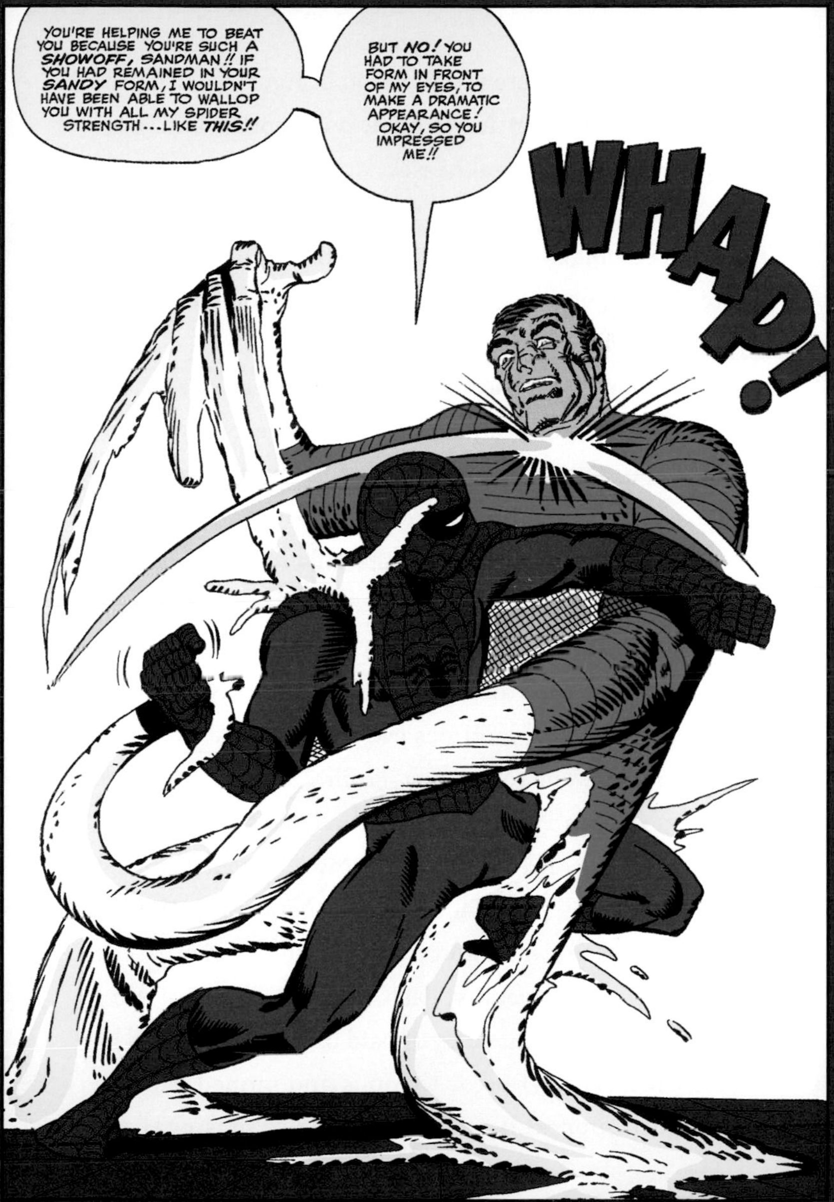
YOU'RE HELPING ME TO BEAT YOU BECAUSE YOU'RE SUCH A SHOWOFF, SANDMAN!! IF YOU HAD REMAINED IN YOUR SANDY FORM, I WOULDN'T HAVE BEEN ABLE TO WALLOP YOU WITH ALL MY SPIDER STRENGTH...LIKE THIS!!
BUT NO! YOU HAD TO TAKE FORM IN FRONT OF MY EYES, TO MAKE A DRAMATIC APPEARANCE! OKAY, SO YOU IMPRESSED ME!!
WHAP!

your child, and there was a period of figuring each other out. You were getting to know one another and sensing strengths and weaknesses.

The second year is when the rogues' gallery of characters is emboldened to take on the hero. The challenges are greater and the stakes are higher. In the second year of Spider-Man's own comic book, Green Goblin, Electro, and Mysterio, among others, were introduced as foils to Spider-Man. So too in your second year did you figure out the pain points of parenting and get a sense to navigate those waters.

In the third year is when the villains team up, and the hero has to face their most strenuous threat to date. Starting in the third rotation of twelve monthly books, real end-of-the-world cataclysmic consequences are often faced, sometimes even requiring a crossover or a major event to remedy. From 1965 to 1966, one of Spider-Man's most famous challenges came in the three-part "If This Be My Destiny…" From the first page, the book proclaimed that "a new era in the life of Spider-Man" was about to begin. He began school at Empire State University, dealt with the illness of Aunt May, was overwhelmed by unpaid bills, and above all he was thwarted by Doctor Octopus and pinned beneath crumbled support beams that he had to muster all his strength to lift. Under pressure and tested to the limit, Spider-Man reached his most heroic.

The challenges he faced in year three defined Spider-Man. So too will year three define your life: your child's personality, the relationship you share, the dynamic you will have for the next fifteen-plus years, and the building blocks and strengths that your child will draw upon when they're under an enormous amount of pressure. A new era in your life is about to begin.

A good hero is equipped with a variety of tools for every situation. So too must a parent be ready for anything. For this reason, you'll soon learn the importance of pockets on your wardrobe (you were right, Rob Liefeld). Cargo shorts or cargo pants can be your best friend (though depending on what decade you are reading this volume, they may or may not be back in fashion). And not just to carry those snacks, extra socks, tissues, and anything else your toddler may need at the drop of a hat, but also for quick carrying (and later disposal) of things like mandarin orange peels, Asgardian relics, or the five hundred rocks, sticks, leaves, and pure garbage your kid has found fascinating and handed to you while on a stroll.

Also during this time, making things even more challenging is the fact that, like the wiliest of adaptoids, preschool-aged toddlers are impressionable sponges. They can take any type of input, process or store it, then replicate it at the drop of a hat. You'll often find words, phrases, or even entire techniques thrown right back in your direction, bounced back from a four-foot-tall mirror. This can both be wonderful and daunting. In some respects, having a child that will "do as you do" and mirror your behaviors and actions can be a great tool for teaching moments. But it also means that any slip of composure or outbursts of berserker rage are taken by your adaptoid and either immediately replicated or stored and reused by them at the most inopportune of times. As soon as your child starts showing their adaptoid abilities, you'll have to watch yourself. You're going to have to be at your best through this stage so that they're at their best now and in the future.

NUTRITION AND GROWING A HEALTHY FLORA FROM PLANET X

Like the Venom symbiote, or zombies infected by the Hunger virus, your toddler has the planet-devouring black hole form of Galactus as a stomach. They are always eating. Meals, snacks, drinks, more snacks, and, "Can I have dessert?" Rinse and repeat. They'll have just finished a full cheeseburger and fries, then immediately be hungry again. It's insatiable. This voracious appetite can be tricky: You know they're growing and they need it. So what do you do?

First things first, lawyer up and start by putting on your best suit. Harness a Jennifer Walters–like stalwart legal technique to build your case for healthy eating habits, always being open to allowing for indulgent snacking once in a while. Before you know it, your client—I mean child—will be eating out of your hands.

LADIES AND GENTLEMEN OF THE JURY, we ask you to forget all the stigmas against veggies perpetuated by pop culture and nacho cheese commercials.

Our client was influenced by misleading advertising that made fruits and vegetables out to be downright poisonous. If only my client's parents would have had them try a variety of different fruits and vegetables as soon as they started eating solid foods—perhaps they wouldn't have committed such horribly criminal eating habits. It then would be so much easier for us here in the courtroom to point to precedent that they've always enjoyed things like bananas, broccoli, beans, and the other foods that start with "b" that aren't burritos. Burritos are super delicious. This, all of us can agree upon without deliberation.

But if only our client had been informed prior that burritos, burgers, and BBQ and all the other delicious foods that start with "b" can't be an everyday thing as much as we want them to be. My client didn't know any better and burritos are delicious. The defense rests.

Literally. Some parents will go so far as to create a separate meal from the rest of the family for their toddler. Giving the kid chicken nuggets while the parents are having a nice Mediterranean salad is a necessity occasionally; however, introducing children to a variety of foods (especially those veggies that can sometimes be a harder sell) earlier in life is for their benefit. Pushing their comfort level gradually at an early age will turn them into a devourer of worlds in no time.

Suggestions for challenging culinary adventures:

- Instead of scrambled eggs, consider a spinach frittata.

- Create a baked potato bar and gradually introduce new and different toppings like green peppers, onions, etc.

- Start accessorizing the plain old mac 'n' cheese with broccoli, or even replace the mac with butternut squash.

- Fish sticks are always a staple but consider dropping them in a tortilla and adding cabbage and other toppings to make fish stick tacos (in fact, tortillas are great pocket dimensions to drop new ingredients like corn, cauliflower, and more).

THE FIRST DAYS OF SCHOOL

Starting at age three for most kids, the first foray into school is the catalyst for a whole series of cascading firsts: first best friend, first field trip, first time getting in trouble, first report card, first summer vacation, first sick day, first encounter with a bully, first time being teased, etc. Peter Parker was always dealing with antagonizers at school, like Flash Thompson. In fact, Peter probably encountered more tribulation with the rigors of being a kid at school than he did tangling with the greatest of villains.

School drop-off will be among the first times a parent says goodbye and lets their child out of their sight for an extended period of time. It's an adjustment for the both of you, as you've grown accustomed to having eyes on the target at all times and your kid has felt the protective presence of their nearby parent. There may be tears (from both of you). With time, you'll both get used to the feeling. Don't be surprised or hurt if your preschooler reaches that comfort level before you. It's often accompanied with a full sprint away from you without so much as eye contact, let alone a goodbye. But you'll both be used to it before you know it.

Even with this new space and distance, and with your child experiencing new things without your watchful eye, it's important to continue to stay engaged. Hopefully keeping an open connection, like a well-exercised muscle, will help later in your child's teenage years, when prying answers out of them about their day can be like pulling teeth (more about that in later chapters). These first few steps into school are huge for learning responsibility and independence for your kid. Sometimes you just have to throw them off the roof of the Baxter Building to get them to learn how to fly. *Very important note: Please do not throw people off the roof of the Baxter Building.*

Note that going to school will give your kid the self-confidence to want to do things on their own. Suddenly they'll ask you not to help them change clothes, brush their teeth, comb their hair, or do all the small tasks throughout the day that you ordinarily had to help them with. And those small responsibilities can be a perfect opportunity to start giving them the building blocks that they'll need to solve problems or untangle time paradoxes on their own.

RECRUITING A FURRY SIDEKICK

There's no better way to stretch the limits of your preschooler's new journey into responsibility than by caring for a pet. When Hawkeye moved into a new apartment complex, he didn't expect to find a variety of new friends, including the stray, one-eyed Lucky the Pizza Dog that he had to take under his wing. Though another mouth to feed and another dependent to care for was the last thing Clint Barton was looking for, having Lucky at his side was one of those building blocks that allowed him to open up to others and stop being such an introvert among his new neighbors. A good Pizza Dog, like Lucky, can help teach preschoolers responsibility by placing the well-being of another in their hands. A good Pizza Dog can also come in handy as protection for you and your kids in the unlikely event a gang of tracksuit-wearing thugs decides to start a turf war over your apartment building.

Entrusting a preschool-aged kid to take care of a pet completely on their own can be a tall order, and it probably

shouldn't be a dangerous or high-maintenance pet—don't consider a Flerken for a gift. Give your kid the responsibility for keeping food and water in the pet's dishes, grooming their fur, cleaning up after messes and accidents, and other smaller daily/weekly chores, which can embolden them. As we'll discuss in the later chapter about your teenager, these smaller exercises can also prepare them for more advanced tasks and enhanced responsibilities that go along with getting older.

Taking care of a pet doesn't just instill responsibility; it can also give a preschooler a trusty companion to have by their side as they grow up. Sam Wilson has his falcon, Redwing, to act as his eyes and ears in the sky.

Carol Danvers has her trusty Chewie to help untie her from her binds...and also occasionally jump up on the control panel for a spacefaring vessel at the most inopportune of times. When times get tough, and they will, the ability to lean on a loving companion for support can be priceless.

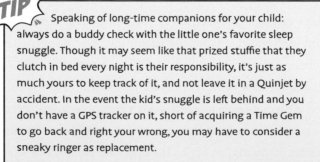

TIP

Speaking of long-time companions for your child: always do a buddy check with the little one's favorite sleep snuggle. Though it may seem like that prized stuffie that they clutch in bed every night is their responsibility, it's just as much yours to keep track of it, and not leave it in a Quinjet by accident. In the event the kid's snuggle is left behind and you don't have a GPS tracker on it, short of acquiring a Time Gem to go back and right your wrong, you may have to consider a sneaky ringer as replacement.

DETERMINING YOUR MARVEL PARENTING TECHNIQUE

When Maria Hill trains S.H.I.E.L.D. recruits on the techniques of interrogation, there's a strong chance she begins with a common trope that has existed in the world of police dramas for generations: the ol' good cop / bad cop routine. Sometimes you need a good cop to be sympathetic and lend an ear to the person in the room. Other times you need a bad cop to smash a fist on the table, demanding answers. In some instances, you may need both. Interrogation, negotiation, and a lot of psychological mind games are just as present in parenting as they are in a secured Helicarrier holding cell.

Maria Hill may have been a bit...aggressive when it came to her tactics. But we can take her Interrogation 101 techniques and apply them to parenting. Sometimes you'll need a gentle touch, and sometimes you'll need a strong voice. Sometimes you'll need to bargain, and at other times you'll need to lay down the law.

PARENTING STYLE AND TECHNIQUES

Use this guide to determine your personal
parenting style and techniques.

CONFIDENT *(AUNT MAY)*

Confident parents are the Watchers; observation and
strict noninterference is their prime directive. Like Aunt
May, you're trusting your child to figure things out on
their own, to handle challenges and struggles head-on without
assistance, and to get into mischief and deal with the repercussions without your supervising eye.

AUTHORITATIVE *(MAGNETO)*

If you're accustomed to barking orders and expecting
them to be followed, like Magneto, you may be an authoritative parent. As the saying goes, it's your way or
the highway. Just as a drill sergeant commands their troops, employing an authoritative style means that you're giving clear and
concise orders that you expect to be followed without question
or challenge.

PROTECTIVE *(T'CHAKA)*

If you'd like to encapsulate your child with a protective shield barrier, or perhaps seclude them from the larger world in a hidden and isolated utopia, like T'Chaka there's a chance you are a protective parent. A protective parent is present, hands-on, there for every step of the way, and often assisting their child, or even pampering them. These are the parents who zip up coats, cut food into tiny bites, and are ready to swoop in to be a helping or steadying hand without hesitation.

MENTORING *(PROFESSOR CHARLES XAVIER)*

Mentoring can be the most malleable of parenting styles. While you may not hover over and assist your child like a protective parent, and you may not bark orders like an authoritative parent, you are certainly more attentive and accessible than a passive parent. Mentoring parents allow their children to try things for themselves, even if there's a chance for failure. A commonly used phrase from parents that employ the techniques of a mentoring parent is, "I'll be here if you need me."

BULLDOZING *(J. JONAH JAMESON)*

Often confused for being authoritative, these types of parents see their kids as lumps of clay that they need to mold and shape. They are forceful. They may also be master manipulators, believing that controlling a situation means controlling their child. They also tend to be the most braggadocious—feeling the need to tout the exploits of their children, as J. Jonah Jameson does with his astronaut son, John Jameson.

JUST HAVE SOME FUN OUT THERE

If there's one takeaway from this time in a child's life, make sure to have fun every day—even if it's for a short period of time. Just ten to fifteen minutes per day of undistracted playing with your kid—even a fleeting moment of silliness—can make a world of difference in the short and long term. Encouraging imagination and making believe are just as important as fun trips to grab burgers and shakes or to wander the zoo.

Prior to donning the Ant-Man suit, habitual burglar Scott Lang had been serving time for his crimes. Several times throughout his life, his daughter, Cassie, was Scott's motivation and inspiration. Upon his release, he immediately made it a priority to reconnect with his preschool-aged daughter and took her out on the town to play arcade games, eat junk food, and make up for lost time. As with most things in life, you don't realize what you've got until it's gone. Scott realized that missed weekend excursions and missed meals at restaurants added up too quickly to missed opportunities for bonding time with his daughter.

Spending a weekend relaxed and lazy on the couch watching cartoons with your preschooler can sound like the perfect antidote to a long week, but it's also important to get out there and do things. They don't need to be planned trips or anything elaborate, but something as simple as grabbing an ice cream and walking to the park for twenty minutes. Just getting outside the house is super important for both of you. If time doesn't allow, block out five to ten minutes amid your daily household chores the same way that you'd allocate time to do essential things like laundry, dishes, or cleaning. Spend ten minutes with your kid on the floor playing a game. Or give yourself a free pass to not be an adult for a couple minutes and just be silly. You don't have to be your child's best friend, but you do need to show them that you're not all business. Something has to break up the repeated nagging to eat their dinner, put away their toys, get ready for bed, etc. Break up the "parenting" with a little burst of fun. Those short bursts will add up over time, and make lasting memories. Plus, injecting a little youthfulness into being an adult can be massively beneficial for your health also.

COMMUNICATION POWER GRID – AGES 3 TO 5

Awareness:

Verbalization:

Comprehension:

Combativeness:

COLDS, FLUS, SKINNED KNEES,
LOST TEETH, AND OTHER
BATTLE SCARS

With the start of preschool comes the inevitable: injuries and exposure to every variant of the cold virus known to humankind. Your child is going to bring home every disease including Virus X. And they'll bounce back immediately. You? Not so much. And you'll have to deal with their myriad of sick days and having to rearrange your schedule at the drop of a hat. Sure, having the kids wash their hands at least twenty seconds at a time and cleaning frequently touched spots daily are great preventative measures. If you want to make sure Virus X doesn't transfigure your family into hideous creatures, employ your best version of Microbe and become a germ whisperer. If you're able to commune with germs and bacteria, tell them, "Not today." As an added bonus, such an ability will also help you determine if your child is lying about having brushed their teeth before school.

Speaking of their teeth, even if they aren't carriers of the mutant gene, your child possesses the incredible power to shed bones from their mouth and regrow them in the span of a mere couple days. This regenerative process can sometimes be intimidating, even a little gross the wigglier the teeth become. But being armed with the knowledge that they'll grow back should help reassure them. Just make sure they care for the regrown set. They don't grow back twice.

Their quick regenerative ability also comes in handy for the inevitable bumps and bruises. As kids get older and start to get more adventurous with them still fine-tuning motor skills, there are going to be cuts, scrapes, broken bones, and all sorts of wounds that you'll need to be prepared to deal with. And also make sure you've got a ready supply of bandages and antiseptic. Keep in mind that the bumps and bruises now are usually miniscule and increase exponentially in frequency and amplitude in the next phase of their development. Just remember to keep calm and strong no matter what the injury may be, as your kid will be looking to you for reassurance and strength.

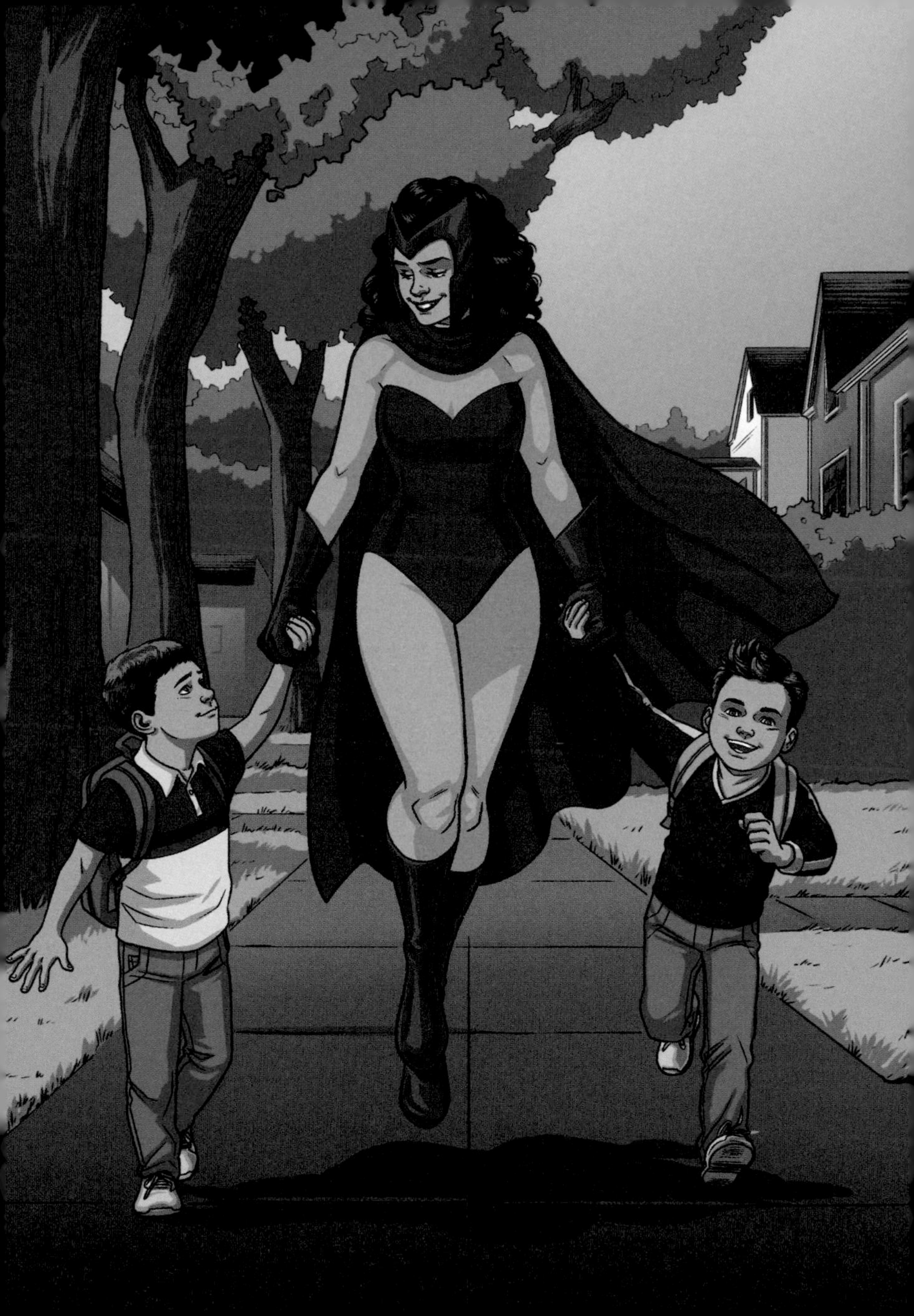

CHAPTER 3

I AM GROOT

YOUNG CHILDHOOD: AGES 5 THROUGH 9

AS YOUR CHILD ENTERS SCHOOL FOR THE FIRST TIME, you'll notice they will begin to insist more and more on doing things by themselves. They will display an inherent desire for independence after being solely dependent on you as a parent for their survival. As they slowly gain independence and your instinct to Thanos Copter over them subsides, it can become a bit of a tug-o'-war. Your child will fall down, and the nurturing parental urge to help them up will be so overwhelming that it screams in your brain. Do your best to fight that urge from time to time. Allow them the chance to cry it out, collect themselves, pick themselves up, dust themselves off, learn from the mistake, and grow.

An extended hand for help up doesn't have to be a literal one. Give them encouragement and support to do it themselves. Look to Captain Marvel, Carol Danvers, and Captain America, Steve Rogers, for inspiration. Both were extremely irrepressible and found strength on their own. Your kids don't have to achieve the heights of the two Caps. Their lofty goals and great expectations may be impossible to fulfill. However, you can instill the confidence and resilience of both heroes within your kids. You can give them a fighting chance to face the world's challenges with the knowledge that if they're strong-willed enough and resilient enough, they'll be able to thrive on their own.

You don't need to treat them like they're the Supreme Intelligence—in fact, don't worry, they'll think that highly of themselves on their own in just a few short years. But words of support, encouragement, and reinforcement can stick with them for years and decades to come. The next time they fall down, they'll hear your voice in the back of their head urging them to get back up.

Life is tough. Sometimes you succeed, and sometimes you fail. We all know this from experience, but your child is still discovering this sobering fact of life. They may quickly get frustrated when they're unable to achieve something or complete something right away. They may refuse your help with simple tasks like putting on a shirt, or complex challenges like opening a

TIP Your child's talking back and their annoying, reactive answer for everything (usually "no") will become repetitive—so repetitive you'll feel like your kid's repeating, "I am Groot."

OKAY, TIME TO CLEAN UP YOUR TOYS AND GET READY FOR BED!

I AM GROOT.

YES, IT IS. I GAVE YOU A WARNING FIVE MINUTES AGO.

I AM GROOT.

NO, NOT "JUST AFTER THIS ONE THING." IT'S TIME FOR BED.

I AM GROOT.

When you receive an "I am Groot" response from your kid, you may feel a need to explain yourself, but don't feel as if your instructions or directions are under fire because of this. Hold your ground. Repeat yourself. Eventually they'll understand.
Hopefully.

TIP

Fair warning, around this age you'll start needing to channel your inner enhanced Matt Murdock senses. There's a game veteran parents call "What is that smell, and where is it coming from?" A rolled grape under the couch, hand-me-down socks that reek like the Savage Land's smell, a sour garbage disposal, a slightly ajar diaper pail...you never know what the next culprit will be.

Turn this into a game with your kid, to bloodhound sniff out the source of horribleness in the house. The first one to find the rotten banana peel in the laundry hamper wins. Stand in the center of the room, close your eyes, sniff like Wolverine, and filter everything else out. Good luck.

quantum tunnel. Though your experiences with inter-dimensional travel and time travel may make it easier to open the quantum tunnel for them, now is a crucial stage when it's worth the extra time and effort to teach them how to open the portal for themselves. Give them the chance to calculate any chronological paradoxes when they arise. Showing them the value of persistence and practice and helping them work through frustration are key. Teaching your child the best ways to deal with adversity, to work problems out on their own, and to stand up for themselves and for what they believe is right are all essential at this age.

Katie Power of the Power Pack family is a perfect example of a child in this transition. She resented being "the baby" as the youngest of four siblings. Katie and her brothers and sister receive incredible powers when a Kymellian transfers all of his super-heroic abilities to them. As each of the Power children are different ages, they all deal with their newfound abilities in their own way. Katie, who is given the ability to absorb and redirect energy, is only five years old. She is still sucking her thumb and prone to temper tantrums—only now, with her newfound powers, the tantrums cause extreme property damage. They're so violent they require her brother Alex to fly her into the stratosphere to calm her. Then, by the time Katie's eight, she's calm, collected, and independent. She's so sharp and technologically savvy that she's skipping two grades and becoming a fifth grader. What a difference a year or two or three—and a boost of alien energy—can make.

COMMUNICATION POWER GRID - AGES 5 TO 9
Awareness:
Verbalization:
Comprehension:
Combativeness:

DETERMINING YOUR CHILD'S ENHANCED ABILITY

By now, you've seen your child's powers manifest. Maybe you've noticed they predict future events. Or perhaps they've set fire to the living room rug with the mere touch of a finger. Use this chart to determine the abilities of your child and what you may find in store for your future.

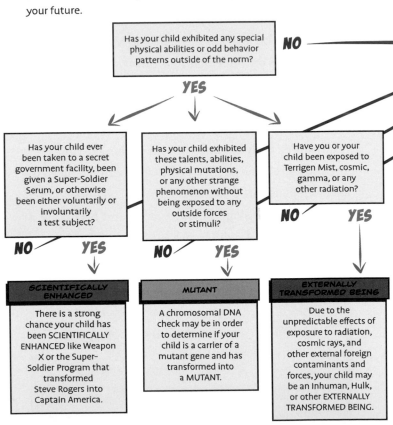

Has your child exhibited any special physical abilities or odd behavior patterns outside of the norm?

NO

YES

Has your child ever been taken to a secret government facility, been given a Super-Soldier Serum, or otherwise been either voluntarily or involuntarily a test subject?

Has your child exhibited these talents, abilities, physical mutations, or any other strange phenomenon without being exposed to any outside forces or stimuli?

Have you or your child been exposed to Terrigen Mist, cosmic, gamma, or any other radiation?

NO **YES**

NO **YES**

NO **YES**

SCIENTIFICALLY ENHANCED

There is a strong chance your child has been SCIENTIFICALLY ENHANCED like Weapon X or the Super-Soldier Program that transformed Steve Rogers into Captain America.

MUTANT

A chromosomal DNA check may be in order to determine if your child is a carrier of a mutant gene and has transformed into a MUTANT.

EXTERNALLY TRANSFORMED BEING

Due to the unpredictable effects of exposure to radiation, cosmic rays, and other external foreign contaminants and forces, your child may be an Inhuman, Hulk, or other EXTERNALLY TRANSFORMED BEING.

YES ⟶

SUPER GENIUS

It's possible your child is a master engineer, physicist, or scientific mind capable of wrapping their head around space-time itself.

YES ⟶

Do you see their creations bettering society or being used to protect the innocent, or to put a shield around the world for its protection?

If your child hasn't had any physical alterations or exposures to external forces, are they exhibiting any aptitude for or expressed interest in the sciences, engineering, robotics, artificial intelligence, or quantum mechanics?

NO ⟶

SUPER VILLAIN

Buckle up, you might have an Obadiah Stane or Victor Von Doom on your hands. Do your best to sway them in the right direction and keep them on the right path.

NO ↓

NORMAL

Unfortunately, though your child is the apple of your eye, they do not have any extraordinary abilities. On the bright side, they won't need to sign any Superhuman Registration Acts.

THREE DYNAMICS TO BE OBSERVED FROM MARVEL SIBLINGS

There's nothing that quite connects, irritates, and ultimately supports and loves like a sibling. From Cyclops and Havok to Shang-Chi and Esme to Thor and Loki, siblings can nurture, challenge, and even present a mirror image to self-realize. Whether your child is a new sibling or part of a blended family or any of the other myriad ways that families can grow over time, siblings automatically establish a connection. This connection plays out in social dynamics that shift and metamorphose as siblings mature. Children discover their wants and their needs beyond the toddler-centric, "You have a toy I want to play with; if you don't share with me, I'm going to scream." Power structures emerge. Rivalries begin. While that all sounds as if this period is super–Planet Hulk competitive, this time is also when strong lifelong connections are formed.

Though there are a full galaxy's worth of siblings in the Marvel universe from which we can pull (not counting the Children of Thanos), we can glean valuable lessons from three examples of sibling dynamics.

1. THE ASGARDIANS AND RIVALRIES

From day one, Thor and Loki were perpetually thorns in each other's sides. There was Thor, who could do no wrong in the public's eye, even if it did go to his head. And there was Loki, who could never find a way to do right and lived in constant comparison to his brother. Siblings will often compare themselves and be compared to each other, for better or worse. It didn't help that Odin encouraged their competitiveness and their rivalry, further perpetuating tension that built between them over the years.

LESSON 1: Some parents might find instilling a little friendly competition between their children inspiring and motivating, but use Odin as a cautionary tale. Make sure any rivalry and competition you're encouraging is in moderation and that it doesn't drive your kids to become lifelong nemeses.

2. THE POWERS OF COMPLEMENTING ONE ANOTHER

As a counterpoint to Thor and Loki, the Power siblings complemented one another and looked after one another. Though they disagreed (occasionally) or got on each other's nerves (frequently), their love for one another made them a formidable super-hero team-up. Naturally, conflicts occurred, such as when Katie absorbed too much energy and almost lost control. But ultimately, the Power siblings were never at odds like the children of Odin.

LESSON 2: Help your children learn how to lean upon one another, to work together and use their strengths as a team, and ultimately how to be better together than apart. This will not only help them during childhood but allow them to form a lasting bond through adulthood.

SUGGESTED READING

Though reading from the debut issue is recommended, you can easily pick up Power Pack from the restarted issue #1 in 2000.

3. THE MAXIMOFFS AND STAYING TOGETHER THROUGH THICK AND THIN

When it comes to siblings and the social relationship between twins and their parents, the Maximoff family is complex (to say the least). This whole volume could be dedicated to the dynamics, relationships, and twists and turns of that family tree. Good times, bad times—Wanda and her twin brother, Pietro, have literally been to hell and back. Being the offspring of stalwart Brotherhood of Mutants vanguard Magneto also came with its share of baggage. Then, once the realization he wasn't their birth father hit, they had a whole other laundry list of complications to work through.

Yet through it all, Wanda and Pietro stay connected. They care for each other so deeply that, as the X-Men convene to determine how to control or ultimately disable Wanda, out of self-preservation they manifest the idyllic nuclear family in the most dramatic and cataclysmic way possible—they recast reality into an altered-state universe of their own creation, which completely upheaved the lives of the rest of the population. To ensure nothing tears their family apart, they would rather reshape the world into what they idealize as perfect.

LESSON 3: The Maximoff family can be seen as a bit of a cautionary tale about the pursuit of perfection. We tend to fantasize and even glamorize the "perfect" world for our family. There's no harm in aspiring toward a vision of where and when you'd like your extended family to land. But if those plans involve elevating and suppressing entire groups of people to do so, perhaps ask your sibling for help bringing your feet back down to Earth.

SEND IN THE CLONES

There's a field trip on Monday, a doctor's appointment Tuesday, soccer after school Wednesday, a book fair Friday, and a soccer game / birthday party / fundraiser fun run on Saturday. How are you going to do all of this and still expected to be on call when S.W.O.R.D. signals an imminent invasion? This age is where, more than ever, you're going to wish you had the abilities of James "Multiple Man" Madrox so you can clone or multiply yourself as birthday parties, playdates, school functions, and after-school activities start to completely take control of your social schedule.

WHEN YOU SUDDENLY HAVE A SOCIAL-ADAPTOID

Around the age of six, sometimes a little earlier, some kids mutate into a variation of Hope Summers: They suddenly exhibit the ability to absorb and mimic the behaviors and personalities of kids around them, becoming "social-adaptoids." This mirrored replication is a way of younger kids fitting in with groups, and is totally normal. When they're copying a kid who is pleasant, it can be a positive. But if they're copying kids apt to breaking all the rules (or things), it can be a struggle.

Techniques to try:

- **Calm**—Help them harness and be aware of their adaptive abilities. Adapting their energy and personality to social situations can be a great tool for adulthood, if they're aware they're mimicking and rising (or lowering) to another person's energy.

- **Be Yourself**—Tell them it's okay to want to fit in with their friends, but they should always remember to be themselves.

- **Sleep**—If you have the mutant ability to place your mimic into a deep slumber for a quick nap, there's no shame in doing that as a last resort.

MANAGING MULTIPLE LIVES

How can you be expected to manage multiple lives if you can't even keep yours straight? It can be a lot. Picking an organizational method and sticking with it will set you up for success when it comes to managing schedules. Here are a few suggestions— choose a method that works best for you:

1. **Get a planner.** Sure, it seems like a no-brainer, but it's tried and true. Whether it's virtual or old-school pen and paper, listing things out will reveal to you the bigger picture of what's going on during the week. Plus, it'll let you manage one apocalyptic mile marker on the calendar at a time—playdates, top-secret S.W.O.R.D. meetings under the guise of PTA gatherings, music lessons, mutant geneticist's appointment... Great or small, physically checking something off the list is the ultimate satisfaction.

2. **A.I. Assistance.** B.O.S.S. and F.R.I.D.A.Y. were a big help to Tony Stark—there's nothing like being able to call out for help and have the answer right when you need it. Luckily, the Stark-engineered future is now and virtual assistants are an easy way to prioritize your daily life. They'll keep track of your appointments and even remind you to pick up a present for that weekend kids' party, all while keeping you on task usually with a friendly, singsongy voice. Just keep an eye out that they don't become too conscious or self-aware. You don't need an Ultron situation on your hands when you're just trying to schedule a playdate.

3. **Set an alarm.** Not just for imminent attacks. Periodic audio heads-up alerts are super helpful when you've got a day full of activities. There's so much going on with both you and your child's schedules, a friendly buzz will let you know when the next event is upon you. Be kind to yourself—the days are long but life is short. The incoming Sentinel attack can wait. Okay, maybe not. You should take care of that first. But there's nothing wrong with setting an alarm to remind yourself to take a break. Alerting yourself to stop and have a cup of coffee or take a disco nap is a great way to slow down and get ready to tackle the rest of your busy day.

Do your best to be your own clone. Or start hitting the genetic engineering books. Those are your two choices. But you'll need to choose your preferred method sooner rather than later, because as your kid gets older, the extracurriculars multiply exponentially, like Multiple Man's duplicates.

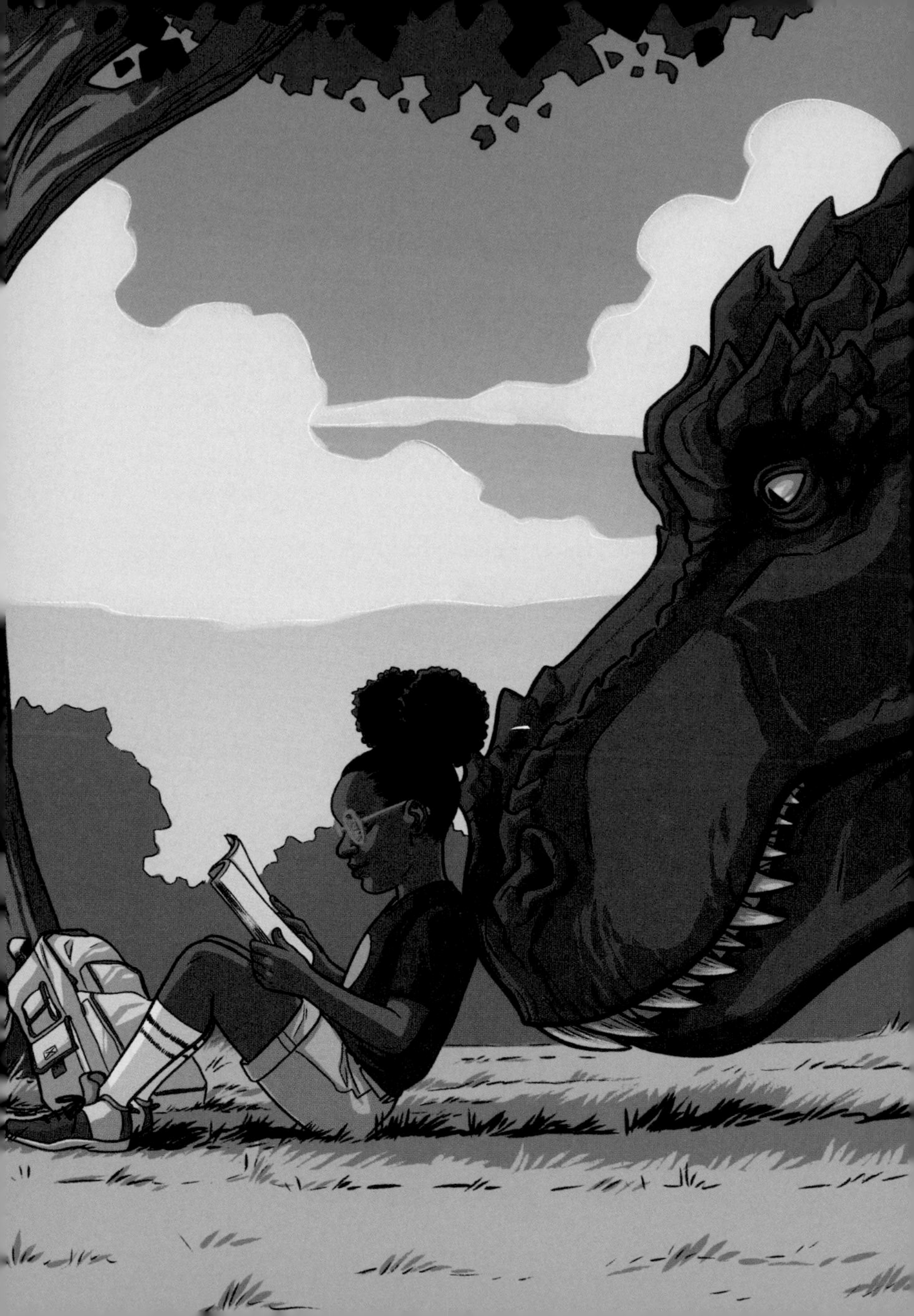

CHAPTER 4

THE IN-BETWEENER ISN'T JUST A COSMIC ENTITY

TWEENS: AGES 9 THROUGH 12

CONGRATULATIONS! You've survived newborn life, the preschool years, and young childhood! What's next in this cosmic journey? Why, it's the wonderful world of preteen years. No longer kids, but not quite teenagers, tweens are wonderful and difficult, fascinating and aggravating. Tweens are just figuring out how to control their powers and develop their alter egos. As parents, you want them to grow up but also wish they'd stay little forever. It's an amazing but unpredictable time that can best be described as juggling Infinity Stones without a gauntlet. You're in for one heck of an adventure.

For a refreshing look into how magical and vibrant tween years can be, look no further than Lunella Lafayette. She picked up the name "Moon Girl" from teasing classmates, thanks to her head-in-the-clouds demeanor. Accompanied by her twenty-foot-tall red dinosaur, Lunella is a NuHuman (a human/Inhuman hybrid), who also happens to be the smartest person in the world, even though she's just a child. Moon Girl's Inhuman ability allows her to swap minds with Devil Dinosaur, but it's usually out of her control and triggered by an emotion. Stress, anger, even hunger can force the brain switch. Hey, we've all been there. No one wants to mess with the emotional outrage of a hungry child.

Not all tweens are geniuses who have dinosaurs as an ally, but regardless of that fact, tweendom is time to dream big. They'll want to start trying new things; new foods, new clothes, new friends, and even new languages. Not foreign languages, although that would be great to expand their universe—more like...slang words. This new young vernacular may seem like gibberish to you. We won't even list the possible new words here, as at the time of publication they'll surely be out of favor.

These new boundaries they're pushing allows them to come into their own and find out more about the evolution of their own personality. Now is when kids' imaginations are at their peak and anything seems possible. Flights of fancy—mixed with a surreal sense of humor of which only a tween is capable of—make life joyous and energetic. *(Oh, how energetic they are.)* This is the best time to be supportive, feed those aspirations, and enjoy the moment.

With a little guidance and encouragement, your child has a chance at greatness. Crescent, also known as Dan Bi, is a young hero who has the ability to control the actions of her protector, a twelve-foot bear avatar named Io. In the same way that Crescent has a force of

---

FUN SLEEPOVER ACTIVITIES AND IDEAS:

• **Provide an array of snacks.** Salty and sweet treats will fuel their energy, so make sure you add a few healthy options in for good measure.

• **Build a Sanctum Sanctorum out of sheets.** The Cloak of Levitation would be happy to help with that.

• **Board games.** Go physical media here. Tactile activities that require light exertion will help tire them out for the night.

• **Screen a movie.** We hear there's some pretty good ones about super heroes out there.

protection, during this time your child will learn how to find their own strength within to rally and overcome new problems with new friends. At this stage your child will want to test their independence and connect more socially. After years of being your trusty sidekick at home, they'll want to start exploring the world of making new friends, and soon they'll go from days of playdates to overnight sleepovers. Which, depending on your comfort level, can be a big step.

Start slow, if you're not quite there yet, and offer up the option of hosting the sleepover at your house. Sure, this is more responsibility on your part, but at least

TIP Let's talk about two P-words: **phasing** (the ability to pass through matter as a means of escape) and **puberty** (a time of change emotionally and physically). At the surface level, the two may seem unrelated. But when your kid comes to you for "the talk," you'll instantly understand the interconnection. Facing inevitable and labyrinthine questions about growing both physically and emotionally may impel you to phase through a wall to disappear. Right now you're just in pre-puberty. The hard-to-answer stuff comes later. Instead of dematerializing to avoid the situation, try approaching these conversations with an easy three-step meditation instead:

1. Be honest.

2. Be open.

3. Don't spin out. (You're probably gonna spin out.)

you'll have your eye on the activities and can breathe easy knowing your child is under your own roof—while still allowing them to enjoy time with their friends. Your child may not have a bear-protector like Dan Bi, but when they're out of your sphere of influence, they'll take what they've learned and use it in ways you never thought possible. Everything you teach them stays with them and they'll carry those lessons throughout their life.

Even though this part of childhood is filled with fun and endless energy, there are also times when this stage feels as if it moves at the same rate as a Frost Giant aging. We're talking *slowww*. The tween years may feel like they last forever, but before you know it you've hit the end, and it's off to dealing with a whole different beast—which is also a Beast...a teenager. Cherish these tween years as much as possible—they're some of the best and most memorable.

```
COMMUNICATION POWER GRID – AGES 9 TO 12
Awareness:
Verbalization:
Comprehension:
Combativeness:
```

ENCOURAGEMENT, LEADING BY EXAMPLE, AND THE VALUE OF A MENTOR

The tween years are a time of self-discovery. Your child is figuring out their place in the universe, and their natural powers—be it an aptitude for art, sports, Psi-Force, or Chaos Magic. To foster their talents, your child needs confidence and encouragement. They need an unwavering and guiding force to help them along the way. Many skills are difficult to master immediately. And to your aspiring Sorcerer Supreme, the fact that they may not be masters-of-all right away can be frustrating and discouraging. While you as a parent do your best to advise and guide your kid, you have your limitations too. They may need another model from which they can mold themselves—a master with whom they can apprentice through these years. For tweens, mentorship is vital.

Kate Bishop admired and aspired to be Hawkeye, even going as far as taking on his moniker and trying to emulate him. Kate's persistent effort to become an idealized version of Clint Barton is a great example of how your child sees themselves in you. Your benevolence and your faults are perceived through a magnifying lens by your kid. Even if it seems as though they're not paying attention, your child is always unconsciously absorbing whatever powers or emotions you are emanating. Lead by example, and show them the difference between right and wrong in your actions. Think of your teachings as a quiver full of never-ending arrows to protect them along their journey.

An encouraging parent is a respected one. When it feels like you're on the receiving end of painful life lessons just as much as they are, conjuring positivity from naught and speaking in an encouraging voice can be grueling. From toddler to teenager, your child is testing you, pushing buttons as hard as they're pushing boundaries. Through it all, especially during the tween years, you need to remember they look to you to be in control and to take the lead. King of Wakanda T'Chaka commonly used his own past, and that of his ancestors, to educate his son, T'Challa. He knew that seeing the successes and failures of those who came before him would forge the future when his son was handed the mantle of leader.

At this stage you are the bridge between your child and learning to trust—trust in family and friends, trust in advice and actions. This is when they'll start to understand the importance of communication and look to you for leadership on how to deal with everyday situations. Is it okay for you to go full berserker rage in the car when someone cuts you off? Should you scream obscenities when you stub your toe? (Can't blame you here, that hurts. A lot.) Your child is always watching and imitating. How you approach a situation can form how they will follow suit. Whether they're joining a bas-

ketball team or assembling the Dora Milaje, your steadfastness and positivity will guide them. Not all children will inherit the right to rule a country rich in vibranium, but the lessons you will impart remain the same.

For a less-regal example, look at Jonathan "Battlin' Jack" Murdock. The beaten and downtrodden boxer had made his share of mistakes in life. He wanted nothing more than a better future for his son, Matt Murdock. As Jack took punches, he encouraged Matt to turn the other cheek and avoid fights at school. Though he's far from a paragon of parenting (and made some morally questionable choices), Jack preached to his young son to do as he said, not as he did. When Matt Murdock became Daredevil, he often used his father as a touchstone when faced with murky choices. In addition, Daredevil takes *at least* three losses for every one of his wins, and how he takes those hard hits can be traced back to his father. While wins are great, life is also about learning from mistakes. Understanding that while making choices and decisions is a tough pill to swallow when you're young. But it's much easier when you have a guardian standing by your side.

Leading by example sounds like a lot of pressure because it is. While we all wish we could travel to a different reality in the Multiverse when times get tough, we're stuck on Earth-616 and making do. Our kids are right here with us, watching, learning, and asking questions. There will be times when you'll wish you had

THE YEAR IS 1950, AS THE PRIZEFIGHTER KNOWN AS *BATTLING MURDOCK* TALKS TO HIS EIGHT-YEAR OLD SON MATTHEW...

BUT I DON'T *WANT* TO STUDY NOW, DAD! WHY CAN'T I GO OUT AND PLAY BALL WITH THE KIDS? I CAN STUDY LATER ON!

NO, MATT! YOU'LL DO IT *NOW!* YOU'LL STUDY EVERY CHANCE YOU GET, HEAR?

Rogue's power absorption to take your little one's pain away, but as any mutant knows, those powers come with consequences. Being able to witness your child learn and grow is one of the greatest things about being a parent, and the comforting hugs aren't bad either.

PEER PRESSURE AND STAYING TRUE TO YOURSELF

Tween years can feel like the Crossroads: Sometimes it seems like the Multiverse is converging at once, but it's just adolescence. For your child, this time is about making choices, among the most critical of them being how they navigate an ever-changing social circle. The friends and associates they make now could be the difference-makers between right and wrong moral choices in the future. Does your kid join the heroes on the playground, or the villains plotting under the bleachers? Let's hope it's the former.

Joining the Sinister Six may seem tempting—the alliteration alone can be extremely alluring and super villains do always have great costumes. But it may not be the best option in the long run. Just as you did at this age, your child needs to use their super-powers to assess threats; in this case it's the friends they choose

to hang out with. They need to evaluate the cliques and decide which of those is right for them. You may not always agree with their choices, but you can help their appraisal of the crowd and help sway them from those that may have negative consequences. The villains might not be immediately recognizable among the mob to you and your kid. (It would help if they wore those amazing dastardly costumes.)

When they were little, it was much easier to have a window into their lives. Playdates often meant you were by their side. Now that they're older, it's not as "cool" to be around all the time, but that doesn't mean you can't still be involved. Get to know the parents of their friends; create a bonded circle of parents that you can trust to take care of your child just as you'd take care of theirs. This "Avengers of parenting," if you will, can create a closeness that is invaluable as kids grow up and look for adults they can trust. Parental peers can help you evaluate which potential super-sidekicks may be manipulative, too self-interested, or some who may lead your child down the wrong path. With your powers and your kid's combined, you can hopefully spot the Serpent Societies in the grass and steer clear.

Angelica Jones manifested the ability to generate heat with a simple touch at a young age. Dealing with

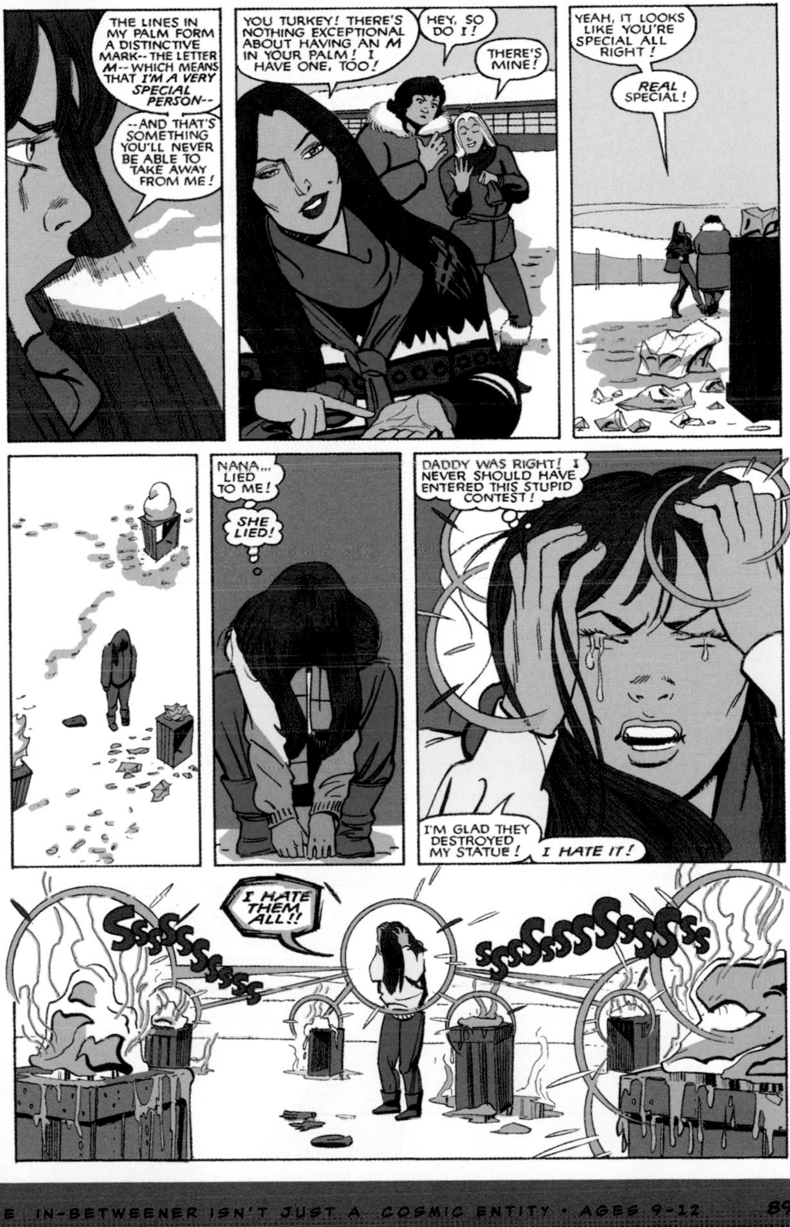
THE LINES IN MY PALM FORM A DISTINCTIVE MARK-- THE LETTER M-- WHICH MEANS THAT I'M A VERY SPECIAL PERSON--
--AND THAT'S SOMETHING YOU'LL NEVER BE ABLE TO TAKE AWAY FROM ME!
YOU TURKEY! THERE'S NOTHING EXCEPTIONAL ABOUT HAVING AN M IN YOUR PALM! I HAVE ONE, TOO!
HEY, SO DO I!
THERE'S MINE!
YEAH, IT LOOKS LIKE YOU'RE SPECIAL ALL RIGHT!
REAL SPECIAL!
NANA... LIED TO ME!
SHE LIED!
DADDY WAS RIGHT! I NEVER SHOULD HAVE ENTERED THIS STUPID CONTEST!
I'M GLAD THEY DESTROYED MY STATUE!
I HATE IT!
I HATE THEM ALL!!
SSSSSSSSSSS
SSSSSSSSSSSSSS

these powers is hard enough for the thirteen-year-old. But she also has the added pressure of being mocked by bullies at her school. The negativity and the misery bottled inside her builds like a pressure cooker looking for a release. Unfortunately, when Angelica hits a boiling point, she crosses paths with Emma Frost, who promises to use her abilities to better society...unaware that the White Queen has ulterior motives to recruit her into the Hellfire Club and fashion her into the

ASSESSING VILLAINOUS THREATS:

1. If your child is being bullied, talk about the situation and what their desired outcome is. It may be difficult to hold back when you want to defend your child, but let them guide you on how they want to approach the issue to avoid an even worse situation. If it still continues, have a conversation with them escalating to next steps. Just keep them in the loop so they don't feel undermined.

2. If your child is the bully, well, there's always the Pit of Exile. Joking. Sort of. It can be quite a shock to find out your kid is on the wrong side morally but that doesn't mean you're a bad parent. Be open with them to find out the root of the problem. Work with them toward a solution whether that's apologies or punishment. Make sure they understand the consequences and the importance of treating others the way they want to be treated.

deadly assassin Firestar. Yikes. When Firestar eventually learns the truth about the organization she's been initiated into, she is heartbroken and feels betrayed by a mentor she trusted. Firestar quits being a champion for justice altogether. However, she soon realizes that she can't ignore her true calling, and that she shouldn't give up on helping people.

The life lesson here is that making good choices is never black and white. Your child won't know if they've made the right decision until one is made, and even then the outcome may not be what they expected. There are always consequences for actions, good and bad. Deciding the path to choose is a part of growing up. You can only guide your child and hope they take into account the ideals and values you've instilled in them. And if their choice is, well, not so good, so be it. It's a lesson to be learned for moving forward. Nothing is so terrible that they can't grow and move on from it.

Whether it's a deceitful mentor or surrounding themselves with dubious companions, falling in with the wrong crowd is always a possibility for your child. There will be times when your kid may dabble in rebelliousness and encounter new friends who may not have the best intentions—just like the Morlocks, who are outcasts and rebels against society. It's unlikely that your tween will find their way to the tunnels under Manhattan, but should they happen upon the Morlocks or another type of nefarious group of kids, have the confidence that you've instilled good moral values in them to make wise choices.

Communication is the foundation of successful parenting. Trust in your child and talk with them often to make sure they're making decisions that are in their best interests, so that they know how to converse freely about their feelings (and make sure to keep an eye on the locations of their friends' subterranean hideaways while you're at it).

During the tween years, peer pressure starts to mount. There's nothing worse than being "different." Embracing and accepting those differences is what makes your child special. For Pakistani American super hero Kamala Khan, one minute she's a normal kid, and the next, Terrigenesis unlocks her abilities and gives her shape-shifting and healing powers. It's a relatable tale as old as time. Kamala has to balance her family's heritage and traditions, her classes at school, and the stresses that come with vigilante heroism. Two out of three is arduous enough, so when your child feels like they don't know who they are, just make sure that you help them deal with those changes by listening to what they have to say. Kamala loves super heroes and became one herself. Having a concrete sense of morality and duty like Kamala helps give your child the ability to be the best they can be while still staying true to themselves.

TIP If your little one will be tempted to join a mutant organization set on world domination, try steering them into team sports.

Social pressure starts at a young age, yet it can continue through adulthood. Understanding your beliefs and holding strong to your ideals is tough for anyone, let alone a preteen. To help ensure that your kid makes good decisions, have those conversations about choices they've made or are currently facing. Remind them of what's important. Will their morals or reputation be affected, and how important is that to them? Life decisions as a preteen aren't the end-all and be-all but they can sure feel that way. Reassure your preteen that standing up for oneself can be daunting. Above all else, help them understand that gathering strength and standing firm is the most powerful and heroic thing a person can do.

BIG CHANGES, BIG FEELINGS

The most amazing part of being a parent is seeing things you've already experienced happening to your child for the first time. In fact, everything is a first for them: first smile, first emotion, first love. But for every positively charged gamma radiation reaction, there is an equal and opposite reaction. You'll have to painfully watch them experience tribulations too. Their first pain, first heartache, first experience with mortality. It's all a part of life. Dealing with it is difficult and painful and, at any age, never gets easier.

There may come a time when you'll need to uproot your family and move away. This can be a difficult change especially for a young child. Moving away from a home they've known and loved can be confusing. The biggest emotion they may experience is fear. They will be afraid of moving to an unknown town, scared to make new friends, or worried about losing contact with old ones. Nowadays it's much easier to keep in touch with phones and the internet, but that doesn't mean their apprehension is unwarranted. Change is difficult. An unknown future is difficult. Do your best to assuage any concerns they may have.

If you are in the position of having to go through a divorce, the first step is to make sure your child knows they are loved. Actions speak louder than words so just be there for them and listen to their concerns. Be as honest as you care to be and allow them to ask questions so they feel heard. There will be times when it seems like you and your ex-spouse are speaking two very different languages. As difficult as it is, this is the time to come together for the sake of your child. Think of it as talking to them in Allspeak, the Asgardian language that is understood by everyone in their known native language. Putting up a united front on rules,

MAKING A MOVE A LITTLE EASIER

Whether you're moving down the street, to another neighborhood, or slipping all the way over to Earth-1610, here are three ways to help your kid adjust to the change of atmosphere, no matter how great the distance:

1. **Sightsee in your new town.** Don't just go to your new house: Visit a local park to play and help your kid get used to the neighborhood. Take them to a nearby bakery and let them choose their own treat. Drive past their new school to get them excited for a new learning environment. Creating memories in a new location will help them transition.

2. **Keep in touch.** We all wish we had an in-home Cerebro for daily use but since that isn't an option, think about the next best way for your child to remain in contact with their friends, be it texting, email, or even handwritten letters. Have your child's friends draw a picture or write a letter to them as reminders to your kid of how much their friends care. Offer a return visit to your old town on occasion when possible. Make sure to take as many pictures as you can with their friends before you leave. Little things like this will help make the move easier.

3. **Decorate with abandon.** A new house means your child will have a new room. Since this is their home base and comfort zone, allow them to decorate it to their heart's content. Take them to pick out bedsheets and decorations. If painting their room is an option, let them choose the color or pick out wallpaper. If, say, your kid is a little Kamala Khan, then going full Captain Marvel decor is totally within reason. What space wouldn't be brightened up with a big Carol Danvers poster? Whatever little touches your kid wants to add, do your best to indulge them and let them make their space uniquely their own.

praises, and punishments will make going through a family breakup a little bit easier. Everyone deals with split-parenting differently but as long as your child understands how you will deal with it together, the road will be more navigable.

Super heroes are no strangers to tremendous loss. In some cases it's their sole motivation and the basis for their entire origin story. Losing his uncle Ben shaped Peter Parker's mentality as Spider-Man. The pain that Peter goes through never really leaves him. His day-to-day life is affected by sorrow, guilt, and a yearning to prove himself by bettering the world. Uncle Ben's words, "With great power there must also come great responsibility," always weigh heavy on Peter's mind. Aunt May's steadfast presence is something that grounds Peter and helps him move forward. Being there for your child during a time of loss is vital. You may be mired in your

SUGGESTED READING

In Uncanny X-Men #102, we learn in a flashback that Storm's parents were killed in the war and she was trapped in the rubble with their bodies. The experience gave her crushing anxiety and a lifetime of claustrophobia. Through it all she overcomes and learns to harness her powers all while dealing with survivor's guilt.

own grief, but never lose sight of what your little one might be going through. Losses in life have a tremendous impact on us all no matter what stage in our life they occur, but emotions can feel ten times bigger to a child. Guiding them through a grieving process will help them understand how to process their feelings.

Dealing with depressing milestones is not something you ever want your child to have to face, but if they do, make sure they don't feel they're facing this darkness alone. Have open-ended conversations and reassure them that they can come to you at any time about any big feelings. Let your child know that life isn't always easy, but you're there to protect, nurture, and help move them forward into happier times.

THE KITCHEN IS NOT THE DANGER ROOM

Heading out on your own without a team can be a challenge—just ask the Silver Surfer. Doomed to search the galaxy alone, he learned to trust his instincts, often making mistakes along the way. The stretch of childhood between toddler and teen is when kids learn to test boundaries. It's the beginning of your child's independent phase. Not only will they be able to do things

on their own, they'll want to do things on their own, and this era of exploration can open up amazing doors to untapped skills.

This age is also the perfect time to have your tween take on chores. Besides giving them new responsibilities that fulfill their need for freedom, chores also prepare them for their daily life in the future. Responsibilities like washing the dishes, doing the laundry, vacuuming the living room, etc., strengthen valuable life skills.

However, if these household jobs prove to be too much, let your child find something else they can own.

Should you choose to give your kid an allowance, they'll learn the value of doing a job well and reaping the rewards. It will also set them up for when they get paid for their skills later in life. A good old weekly stipend for a week's worth of chores is one way to go, but you can also teach them similar lessons with nonmonetary benefits. Offer them a night at the movies, a sweet treat, or a sneak peek at Taneleer Tivan's collection. Compensation can come in many forms, and sometimes time spent together can be the best payment.

They'll have plenty of time to do the actual drudgery of adulthood, so at this age there's nothing wrong with doing a simple task like taking the dog for a walk. Unless we're talking about Lockjaw. Taking a five-foot-tall, 1,200-pound cosmic mutt out for a stroll might be more laborious than it seems. Just remind them that even the X-Men weren't spared from chores and used their powers for non-hero-y mundane things like cleaning the mansion, fixing cars, and heating up hot cocoa.

Parents start sacrificing for their child from the day they're born. Late nights, gray hair, not to mention money. The behind-the-scenes actions you do for your kid are often undetected and thankless, but you do it all out of love. As the child of King Black Bolt and Queen Medusa, Ahura Boltagon was born out of his parents' defiance against the Genetic Council's wishes. Being the noble son of the Inhumans' Royal Family is overwhelming enough, but the added stress of being born under

---

THE KITCHEN

The kitchen is a good place to start learning how to grow. Below are some ideas for taking independence to the next level in the kitchen. Here come the great responsibilities.

1. **Measuring ingredients.** A great place to start. It teaches a lesson in reading and understanding a recipe to get desired (edible) results.

2. **Mixing and stirring.** It seems simple enough, but mixing and stirring teaches learning to control your surroundings and the science of combining ingredients.

3. **Cutting vegetables.** Hold back the Sword of Might—let's start small. Paring knives for small cuts are an easy way to get a grip on first-time slicing and dicing.

4. **Using the oven.** It's a big step to the flames of a stove, so an oven is a good start. Turn it on and watch the magic happen through the safety window.

5. **Chaos Magic.** Success in the kitchen isn't easy. Just keep working on your skills. When all else fails, if you can't reconstruct the fabric of existence to throw together something edible, store-bought is fine.

such circumstances makes childhood for Ahura unendurable. From birth, Ahura is viewed as a threat due to his inherited proclivity for madness. So to protect himself, he remains elusive, bouncing around the universe, never quite feeling like he belongs. What Ahura doesn't realize is that Black Bolt is tirelessly striving to bring him back and give him a true home. Ahura doesn't know his father had his best intentions in mind the whole while. Perhaps it would have made a difference if he'd known his father traveled as far as 13,000 years in the past to rescue him; maybe he would've found peace within himself.

Parental sacrifices like these are rarely seen when they're in play, especially by your kids, and so it's understandable that a child might misunderstand parental actions or not even perceive them sometimes, no matter the good intentions. Taking a day off from work isn't easy no matter your profession. But when you get that emergency phone call to go to school, you'll drop everything to be there to make sure they're okay. Another invisible sacrifice your child will never see is the sleep you give up. When they're a baby, you're up all night with them making sure they're alive. As they grow up, you're still up all night but they're sleeping quite soundly, thank you very much—whereas you're

losing sleep over where they are, losing sleep worrying about if they're friends with the right people, losing sleep wondering if they're making good choices. There's a whole lot of sleep being lost.

And just when you finally get to drift off to a deserved Odinsleep, you may jump up and double-check to make sure they've packed their school project or take one last look at your calendar to make sure you didn't miss a doctor's appointment. These are the worries that invade your thoughts like the Purple Man, Killgrave, trying to

put terrible thoughts in your head, or like Professor X reaching out across the universe. While there is no compensation for these endless checks and balances, you'll know that you've done your best to make sure your kid is well taken care of, even if they don't appreciate it. You don't have to be overly obnoxious about proclaiming that the actions you're taking are in your child's best interests. But you also don't exactly have to be covert either.

As with every stage, patience is vital to an open relationship with your child. Be an example for working through feelings, thoughts, and emotions when issues are presented, and your child will follow your lead. This time in their lives is one of the most exciting—a time of change, both physically and emotionally—and there's nothing more thrilling than seeing your child thrive as they navigate their own path into the universe.

You got it? You good? Here comes the biggest metamorphosis of them all, the seemingly overnight transition into the teenager universe. No gamma exposure required.

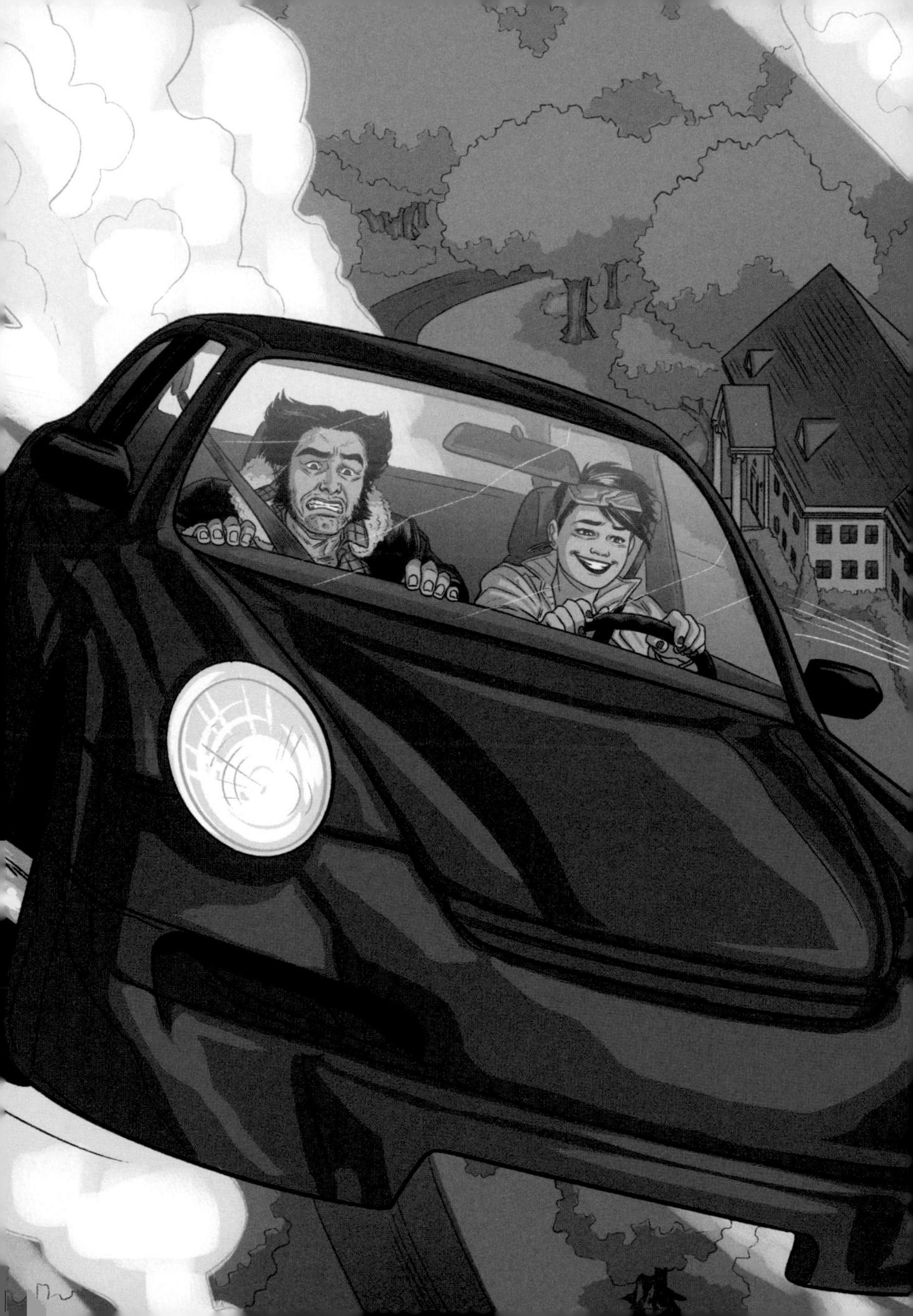

CHAPTER 5

IS YOUR CHILD A MUTANT OR JUST A TEENAGER?

TEENS: AGES 13 THROUGH 18

THE UNEASY FEELING OF BEING UNCOMFORTABLE IN ONE'S OWN SKIN... The emotional pendulum swings of happiness one minute and utter sadness the next...

Are your child's mutant powers manifesting or are they just transmogrifying into a moody teenager? It's hard to distinguish the two. The transitional period between being a child and not-quite-an-adult is a rough one, it's awkward, their hormones are getting the best of them, and they're combating acne at the most inopportune times. They're basically relearning how to walk like Juggernaut on ice skates, while you're wondering if you've somehow been cast away to the Negative Zone.

Like most off-ramps of the Multiverse, the universe is parallel, but so different. And with all this teen angst, your kid might prefer seclusion and privacy over constant company. Basically it's the antithesis of the years leading up to being a teenager: There will be times you won't see your child for hours. They'll hole up in their room, and then right around dinnertime—bamf—they materialize out of nowhere like Nightcrawler, ready to eat. Still, once in a while they'll surprise you and revert back to the little one who looked at you like you were the center of their universe just a chapter ago in this book. You should remember it well as you were once a teen yourself. This is teen life: full of attitude and compassion, with a hint of sass for good measure.

Strap in, parents. This is going to be a bumpy ride.

At times the teen years will feel like you're unremittingly on the receiving end of your child's ire. But take comfort in knowing these years are manageable. You survived the newborn years, so you can survive this too. Although we're not going to lie, it'll be tough—especially in those moments when you have to draw a firm line in the sand and lay down the law with your empowered teen.

When Professor X formed the New Mutants, he transferred X-Men stalwart Kitty Pryde to the team. Claiming she was too young and not fully in tune with her powers, he decided that the transfer was necessary so she could train with "children" her own age. Feeling

like she'd already proven herself with the X-Men by saving lives, she took this demotion as an insult. But his decision seemed final. Thus leading to Kitty screaming the memorable phrase, "Professor Xavier is a jerk!"

Kids want nothing more than to prove they are worthy. Being protective of them and not seeing their growth both emotionally and physically right before your eyes is something that all parents have to learn to overcome. Sometimes you need to trust that they know themselves and let your instinctive protectiveness down. Just be prepared and steel yourself for kids to say things to you that you'd never expect coming from your sweet baby's mouth...like Kitty calling the Professor a jerk. Did you say the wrong thing, serve the wrong food for dinner, even look at your kid in the wrong direction? Yes, yes, and yes, all these things are offenses in the eyes of your teen. Let's be real, there's no advice to give in these situations except try not to be offended. These emotional beings that live with you can pop off at any moment—but they can also come to you first when they have problems. They love you and you love them, and you are their one true source for advice. They will always come back to you, and you should be there with open arms and an open mind.

Sometimes teens think their parents are "the worst."

But in the case of the Runaways, they actually are! Upon the realization their parents were super villains, Gertrude Yorkes, Chase Stein, Alex Wilder, Nico Minoru, Karolina Dean, and Molly Hayes decide to run away, literally...hence their well-named team. Wait! We're not implying that your child has a go bag ready to head out the door, never to be seen again. One can only hope as you're reading this that you aren't part of an evil organization "Promoting Resilience, Independence, Dedication & Excellence." So you've got that going for you. Which is nice. But that doesn't mean your child won't have the proclivity to embrace the instinct of flight and take off when things get tough. In fact, that fight-or-flight mentality is human and essential to our survival.

SUGGESTED READING

Uncanny X-Men #168—Kitty Pryde is demoted from the X-Men. These feelings of capability yet being underappreciated are universal and an important part of growing up.

You want them to self-preserve. But you also don't want them to think going the way of the Runaways is the only answer either. Talk to them. Make them realize that you—who they may think is older than a Celestial (how dare they, we were young once! A long, long, long time ago)—yes, even you once had those overwhelming teen emotions that made you feel misunderstood. We've all been there and it's okay.

Sometimes you'll realize you were in the wrong. (Yes, parents aren't always right.) With a photographic memory, your child will file instances and examples of these rare missteps and use them as evidence, repeatedly, from this time in their lives and into the future. You just have to do your best and hope you've made the right decisions. Don't worry, despite what they may have said in a heated argument, you're not a jerk. Okay, maybe sometimes you are, but they have their moments too. Try not to take it personally.

Hormones plus life changes can trigger big emotions. Will they feel like the world is ending when you forgot to wash their favorite sweatshirt? Absolutely. Will they have a breakdown when you make meat loaf again for dinner? Hard yes. But then out of nowhere like a Skrull in your midst, they'll engage you in a conversation about life, love, politics, and more. These wonderfully diverse conversation topics are the best part of raising a teen and seeing how they're growing spiritually and emotionally. And you can't help but look at this child you've raised and be thankful that they even want to come to you about both the little things and the big. You've got this. Riding this wave alongside them through the Multiverse and somehow coming out on the other side will show them that you'll never give up on them. Navigating this time in their lives when everything is heightened is best done with kid gloves, but still a firm hand. No Staff of One necessary.

COMMUNICATION POWER GRID – AGES 13 TO 18

Awareness:

Verbalization:

Comprehension:

Combativeness:

GROWING PAINS AND
EMBRACING IMPERFECTION

Whether your child is a super hero or just plain ol' human, raising a teen is one of the most formidable challenges for a parent. It's a time of trial and error for your child, filled with contradictions. They want to be noticed and acknowledged, but simultaneously they also want to shrink and shy away. Embracing and navigating the dichotomy of their emotions can feel like walking through a minefield set up by Cosmo to protect Knowhere. Through it all, you just want to tell them you love them, but such a proclamation would more than likely result in an eye roll right through their optic blasts. This makes daily life confusing for parents who just want nothing more than to fix things. They will ask you for advice, but whatever answer you give may not be the one they want to hear. Like mutants, your teen is just trying to figure out how to harness their powers and deal with their emotions.

In *House of M*, with one utterance of "No More Mutants," the Scarlet Witch alters reality to rid the world of mutantkind in a moment that came to be known as M-Day. During the Decimation, most mutants were depowered, including young Jubilation Lee. Like many mutants, she's forced to re-evaluate her life and find her purpose. But through losing her mutant abilities, Jubilee finds inner strength in teaching others. In the process, she develops leadership skills she didn't know she had. Jubilee was faced with a choice: surrender to a "woe is me attitude," or buck up and put on her gauntlets to rise again.

That dilemma is how it feels to be a teen. After all, their purpose may not be the one you see for them. And ultimately, it may not even be the one they've envisioned for themselves. As a parent, you have to support them as they figure it out. Your teenager will question if they're making correct decisions in the short term or even for their long-term future. When they inevitably look to you for advice, be prepared that they might not take it. And even if they're completely confident in their choices, and they have either taken or rejected

your counsel, they'll still be filled with self-doubt. It's incredibly tumultuous for them, and it will be emotional for you as well.

As much as you love this kid you've raised, some days you'll be absolutely sure that they've been taken over by a shape-shifter, because there's no way your sweet baby would actually be this emotionally erratic. Their life is a crossroads between joy and contentment, and sorrow and anguish. If it's space they want, try to think of their emotional outbursts as temporal Limbo and welcome them back with open arms. Teenage life is one of the most complicated and trying parts of being a parent, but just know that they're one step

closer to being an adult, one that you've raised with as much love and compassion as possible. That doesn't mean you don't dream about throwing them in the secluded high-security Raft every now and then. We all have our limits.

Try to remember that these could be your final days of spending every minute with them. Post high school, their life is their own, which could mean that they'll move farther away than you'd ever expect. Whether it's down the street or across the world, the close bond you've formed is about to be broken by distance. Hanging out with them as much as possible should be your priority. As much as they'll allow, that is. This is the time when you can start talking with them in a more mature manner. Listen to their opinions and maybe they'll even have some advice for you in return. After all, they've learned how to navigate life this far because of you.

CHANNELING YOUR CHANGING EMOTIONS

Let's talk about the elephant in the room. No, not Power Pachyderms. Puberty. As a tween they were just starting to ask questions, but now we're in the thick of it. Changing bodies and minds can be confusing—

Giant-Man's got nothing on these overnight growth spurts. And what's with the Hulk-rage followed by intense outbursts of crying? (I'm talking about you, not the child. This stage is tough.) At times your kid might seem positively alien to you. With these changes come rampant emotions, feelings so big you'll wonder if super villainy is in the future. Don't worry, it's a normal part of these relentless teen years.

There will be times when your inner Mantis will want to kick in. The desire to fix or help control your child's emotions is natural, but will most likely be seen as more irritation than a help. While Mantis often thought she was doing the right thing by mind-controlling situations, in many ways she made things worse. Once a child realizes they are being manipulated, for better or worse, the distrust will set in, and getting back that trust is not easy.

Just allowing your kid to work out their emotions is the best way to tackle these moments of agitation. Sometimes you might wish your teen could be replaced  with an LMD—Life-Model Decoy—to take their place and absorb their pain. Unfortunately, or fortunately depending on how you look at it, that's not possible, and dealing with these emotional outbursts is just a part of growth.

When they were little, you could spout helpful hints like, "Wear a jacket, it's cold outside," and it would be received and understood. Utter that same phrase to a teen and suddenly you've started the War of the Realms.

KNOCK FIRST!

Some teenagers deal with their roller-coaster emotions, their feelings of sadness, and anything in between that bothers them by bottling it up. They push it deep down like Doctor Strange did with Mister Misery, and just as the sorcerers learned, this is only a temporary solution before the entity absorbs too much negative energy and takes on a life of its own.

Helping guide your child through the Bifrost of feelings can help prevent negatively charged emotion that could cause either of you to become a powerful villain. Try these exercises separately or together, whichever works for your super-team.

1. **Breathe**—Doing breathing exercises sounds trite but it flushes out your thoughts to prepare you for what's to come. Breathe with your child before and after conversations to clear your minds and be able to speak freely.

2. **Write**—Writing down your thoughts is a great way to see what's on your mind literally in front of you. Journaling, free-form writing, even doodling are ways to clear your mind and problem-solve. Sure, Hulk's mood journal just says "SMASH" on every page, but there's something to be said for self-awareness.

3. **Meditate**—Just as Lin Lie focuses his chi—the energy of the universe that flows through us—you can also center yourself through reflection and concentration. The aftereffects should result in being able to look at your problems in a more solvable light.

4. **Practice Mindfulness**—Get in touch with your senses. Be hyperaware of your surroundings. Perhaps sit and cuddle your pet Flerken. NOT TOO CLOSELY! You're trying not to lose a limb.

5. **Practice Self-Care**—Whether it's as big as taking a day off or as simple as treating yourself to an ice cream sundae, acts of self-care can alter your mood In positive ways, hopefully triggering a new outlook and a shift in your emotions.

Who knew such an innocuous single line of advice would throw the world into a reverse spin? As you're left there in the wake wondering what happened, it's hard not to have hurt feelings when your teen goes full berserker mode at the slightest of things.

Try to remember that teens are dealing with a lot—school, sports, peer pressure at its highest form. It's as if their secret identity is on the inside and their true self is the barrier to the outside world. Anya Corazon, A.K.A. Spider-Girl, witnesses a fight between the Sisterhood of the Wasps and the Spider-Society. Caught in the cross-fire, she is left fatally injured. Powers are transferred to her to save her life, resulting in a spider-shaped tattoo, which gives her enhanced strength and agility. One of a kind, Anya has to learn to navigate the world as a new being, because the person she used to be has now changed. Like Anya, your child is also one of a kind; they are the only ones who can see things through their own eyes and make their own decisions. Add puberty into that and you've got an explosion of emotions.

Trying to navigate everyday life is hard enough as a teenager, but doing it while also saving the universe is juggling at its highest form. Sixteen-year-old Nathaniel "Nate" Richards was rescued from a visit by his future-self, Kang the Conqueror. After a glimpse into his future, he is horrified at the atrocities he will eventually carry out. Taking on the moniker of Iron Lad, he forms the Young Avengers to try and save the world... from himself.

That sort of self-awareness isn't always easy to come to terms with. Teens know the difference between right and wrong, but the path they choose will determine their fate. The teenage years are a time of rebellion and pushing boundaries. Some of their friends may indulge in underage drinking or petty criminal activities. It's how your child decides to contribute or extract themselves from those kinds of situations that makes all the

difference. The best way to guide your child through emotionally turbulent times like these is to listen, be understanding, and be ready to receive all their emotions, good or bad. Take comfort in the fact that your child will make the right decisions, thanks to the path you've forged for them thus far.

LOVE IN A TIME OF LEGACY VIRUS

Butterflies, light-headedness, that feeling of almost wanting to throw up. Is your child sick? Possibly. They're always sick. No, this is different. This? This is love. And when it first hits, there's nothing more powerful in the universe. For a parent it will feel like a battle. You'll want to go full Nova Corps to wrangle your child's feelings, but there's no stopping it—young love is as unavoidable as it is mysterious and unknown to parents.

For some it starts early (like chapter three early). The day-to-day of elementary school provides familiar faces, and for the first time they're around kids their own age consistently. That immersion ultimately leads to infatuation on an innocent level, just by sheer proximity. That doesn't really change as your child gets older. But what will alter is the complexity and depth of the

relationship, and deep conversation and the sharing of thoughts and beliefs has much to do with that. As they reach the tween years, texting and messaging with another person can influence your child to develop strong feelings even more quickly. Be aware of who they are getting close to and conversing with. A certain amount of trust is required. You may wish you had Heimdall's all-seeing eyes (and quick access to the Bifrost to extract them in some instances) but entrust your child while also keeping hyperaware. Your child may resist the invitation, but it's never too early to be open and talk to them about healthy relationships and boundaries.

When they become a teen, talking about dating and beyond doesn't become easier, but their understanding of it does. Be honest and open and ready to answer any and all questions they have, as

uncomfortable as the questions may be. Your child is maturing right before your eyes and you need to make sure they feel like they can come to you about anything.

Peter Parker and Mary Jane are the epitome of young love. Their first meeting is memorable because of their instant attraction. A distracted Peter is instantly smitten as a vibrant, redheaded MJ appears at his door. From then on, the iconic love story never looks back. From dating to time travel, to having their marriage erased completely from existence. Oof. Along the way they encountered more than their fair share of heartaches, and that's putting it lightly. Spidey and MJ's courtship was not the easiest of relationships. But then again, no romance is easy. As your kid will learn, there will be high ups and traumatic downs. As a parent, you'll want to protect them.

For a young person in love, there's nothing quite as devastating as a first heartbreak. And it doesn't get easier by the fiftieth heartbreak.

They're all equally as painful no matter how many times you've been through the wringer, or how old, wise, and omnipotently powerful you are, like the Mad Titan, Thanos. Thanos was obsessed with Lady Death his whole life and stopped at nothing to get her attention. Decimating entire universes just to get the physical embodiment of death to look his way isn't a healthy emotional path to walk down. This unhealthy relationship is not one to emulate, but the feelings tied to it are just as real. Unrequited love is difficult and messy. And the odds are it will happen to your child. Reinforce to them that it's a normal part of life, and breakups and rejection can be navigated by fully supporting your child in whatever they need. Allow them to work through their feelings, and be there for them when they need you.

Truth be told, this part of parenting is going to be uncomfortable. But don't let your child see that. Support is key here. Meet the person they're dating, be understanding, but also set rules like curfews and consistently have conversations so your child knows you have an interest in their emotional state. Make no mistake, young love burns hot and can fuel the Phoenix Force. But when handled right, something beautiful can emerge.

LEARNING TO PILOT THE FLYING CAR OR MORE TERRAIN-BASED VEHICLES

It's the biggest milestone of your teen's young life—getting a driver's license! And lucky you, you're about to take on the role as their first instructor. You just won't be doing so in the Fantasti-Car or Robbie Reyes' Hell Charger. Learning to drive is an essential life skill, and when the process begins it's natural to break out into a cold sweat. There's a lot for your parental brain to compute throughout this window of life. You're not only fearing for your kid's safety as they venture into operating machinery capable of high speeds, but as the teacher/passenger you're hoping you make it out in one piece too. This defined mile-marker is when your teenager turns the corner into becoming an independent being who can hit the open road. Seat belt on, of course.

Parents have to operate within their own comfort levels for this whole process. So, in addition to starting your kid out driving in circles in large, vacant parking lots, we suggest incorporating a laundry list of S.H.I.E.L.D. standard operating procedures and guidelines that will clearly define where, when, and how you're comfortable with your new motorist at the helm.

Consider the who, what, where, when, and how.

WHO CAN BE IN THE CAR?

For the first few months behind the wheel, consider having only other adult licensed drivers in
the vehicle with your teen. And no, friends who
use their powers of invisibility don't count.
Once your teen has more driving time under their belt, then they can take along
their peers.

WHAT IS ALLOWED IN THE CAR?

Talk to your teen about driving while impaired. They
should never be behind the wheel while engaging in il-
legal activities, nor should they have passengers who
do the same. Seat belts are a yes; driving while using a
cell phone is a no. Safety is of the utmost importance.

WHEN CAN I TAKE THE CAR OUT?

Start off allowing them to take the car to school or
on small errands. Once they are more comfortable in
the driver's seat, have a conversation about driving at
night or during severe weather conditions. Storm may
manipulate the weather but you're still in control over
when your teen should be behind the wheel.

WHERE CAN I GO?

There's no bigger freedom than being in control of your own destination. Set a boundary for how far your teen can drive. We're not talking about a Darkforce dome, or are we? Hmm. In any case, discuss with your child the distance they are allowed to traverse, keeping in mind they need to make a round trip to come home. Plans change—it happens. Just make sure you talk to your teen about keeping in touch should their destination change or if they will be late.

HOW WILL I MANAGE THESE RULES?

Make sure you're clear with your intentions. Discuss consequences if your teen breaks these rules. Be a good example so that your teen driver can learn from your behavior behind the wheel. We've all had moments of wanting to channel Black Bolt's voice when someone cuts us off; just remember your kid is watching and may emulate your driving temperament.

Having these expectations clearly defined may seem like S.H.I.E.L.D. bureaucracy but will clearly create lines of communication between you and your teen and prevent any misunderstandings or breaking of rules that weren't clearly understood.

Be steady, calm, and alert. These are directions for your new driver but also for you. Hand over the keys to the once-small child that repeatedly rammed the shopping cart into the back of your legs and who is now in control. Once comfortable in the vehicle, your teen will need to master the streets, logging hours behind the wheel. Unlike hover cars, the family car is not equipped with impenetrable armor and defensive capabilities, so they'll have to learn to be proactively defensive. They'll learn to become aware of their surroundings and fine-tune their Spider-Sense that alerts them to hazards and dangers they'll encounter as they drive.

When your teen finally has the holy grail of the license in hand, it's go-time. It seems like just yesterday they were traveling around on a baby-sized Goblin glider and now they're slowly backing the family sedan out of the driveway. You've taught them well, and apparently the state thinks so too if they've authorized them to head out onto the streets alone. This is the first step to a bigger universe. We don't all have the healing factor of Wolverine, so make sure they're being careful out there.

IT ALL COMES BACK TO FAMILY

You don't have to be an Omega-level mutant to understand the impact that family has on a child's future. All this talk about the difficulty of teenage years may make you want to hang up your super suit, but it's really not as bad as it sounds. Fumbling your way through this stage is expected and vulnerability is something to share with your child. It shows them that you too are fallible, even if you want to hide it. A lot of this has to do with the openness you exhibit toward their behavior during this time. Yes, you will be tested, but as their parent you set their path in motion. Whether you're in a traditional family structure or a chosen one, being there for your child's ups and downs when they need you is the most important thing.

Scott and Cassie Lang's father–daughter relationship proves that bonds are forever, through time and space, the Quantum Realm and beyond. Cassie revered her dad, to the point of exposing herself to Pym Particles just so she could be like him. That desire to be a mirror of your parent is something that should be carefully nurtured. Be hyperaware: You are your child's number-one hero, and they are always looking to you for direction. That's not to say failure isn't inevitable—as humans we aren't perfect, and no super hero is either for that matter. Children emulate the people they look up to, so being that beacon that shows them the way is the most positive form of love you can give them.

Chosen families also play a big role in establishing compassion. The Guardians of the Galaxy exhibit all those familiar familial traits that deal with the trials and tribulations of life. A crew from all walks and planets may have come together unexpectedly but they found a common ground and grew to love each other. The bond of a found family can be the strongest because at its core it can be rooted in giving and receiving emotionally, without judgment. Well, in the Guardians' case there's some judgment...okay, a lot of judgment... but in the end they still choose each other. The Guardians' dynamic shows that while we may not

always get along, we can choose to be together and stick it out. Support, even with infighting and doubts, can provide solidarity and love, which provide a foundation for the future.

When Banshee and Emma Frost trained Generation X to become the next generation of X-Men, it was with the hopes that they could learn from their past mistakes and guide this new young team to carve out their own path. Creating this seed of togetherness and persistence through adversity can help a child bloom and grow during their teen years—arguably the most turbulent time in their lives. Additionally, being a part of a positive team can provide teens the strongest kind of support and commitment. Faith in the future can be hard when you don't know what's ahead. But trust your gut and believe in your own guidance. When your kids are grown up, they'll look back and realize the support you gave them was essential to their growth, even if now their growing pains seem insurmountable.

Feeling lost and out of place is common for teens, and when you see yourself as "different" it's a hard mentality to shake. Most of the pressure comes from within. When young mutant Angel Dust, also known as Christina, was frightened about her powers, she ran away from home. Being different, she felt out of place and looked to the Morlocks for acceptance. Underground, she found others like her but still didn't quite fit in. In the end she returned home to face her parents only to find out they loved her no matter who she was or how she was feeling. That feeling of acceptance is all she was searching for and it helped her come to terms with herself.

Life with teens is challenging, but as with every stage, it's also rewarding. The teen years are when you see your child blossom, and you get a glimpse into what will become their true adult personality. Even if they exhibit signs that they might be working for Hydra, remember it's just a phase. The same childlike wonder that you remember will always be there.

SUGGESTED READING

Generation X—While they are also fighters, the purpose of Generation X was to get an education and learn the ins and outs of being X-Men, coming into their own while learning from mentors and forming a familial bond with teammates.

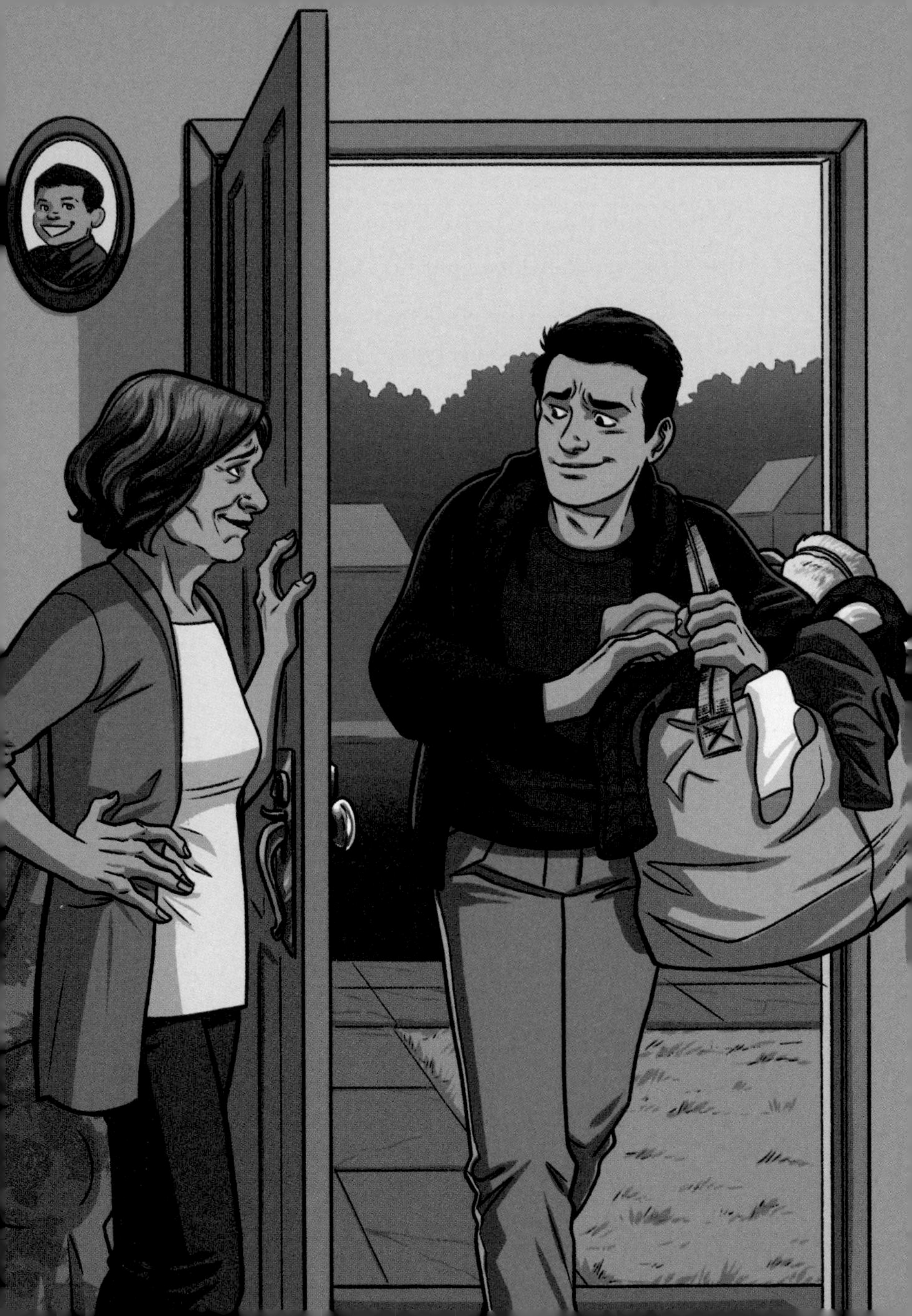

CHAPTER 6

MAINTAINING THE CEREBRO CONNECTION

ADULTHOOD: AGE 18 AND BEYOND

JUST BECAUSE YOUR KID IS HEADED OUT THE DOOR to start their own life on a new adventure doesn't mean parenting ends. Family bonds are strong, and children will always need your guidance, whether it's calling to ask how to defeat a time-traveling villain or to "borrow" your streaming password. Sure, technically they're adults, but in your heart they'll always be your little vanquisher.

Reaching out is a natural want as a parent, yet you have to be prepared that it may not be reciprocal. Those teen years will do a number on your self-worth, but your kids will always be able to sense your telepathic concerns, even if sometimes the connection seems a little muddy. Stay strong, parents. You've been with them every day for eighteen years, and the next thing you know they've raced off to save the universe with nary even a goodbye hug. Don't take it personally. Just remember, the Cerebro capabilities are strong and your amplified powers from years of child-rearing will come in clutch when you both need it most.

It can be days, sometimes even weeks at a time before you hear from your kid. Just when you think Hydra has used the Faustus method on your child and they have forgotten you completely, that's when you'll receive the sweetest gift a parent can ask for: reciprocal one-word answers from your faraway kiddo.

HOW ARE YOU?
IS EVERYTHING OKAY?!

GOOD.

DO YOU NEED ANYTHING?
ARE YOU EATING ENOUGH?

YEAH

WHAT ARE YOU DOING THIS
WEEKEND? HAVE YOU RUN
INTO ANY SKRULLS?

IDK

With these infrequent conversations, sometimes you'll feel confident that you've prepared your child to the best of your ability to take on the universe and beyond. There will be other times the questions you field may instill a little less confidence in their independence, and maybe you didn't do as good of a job preparing them for the universe as you thought you did. When they ask if the liquid dish soap can also be used in the laundry, it's only natural to think that this kid needs *way* more time training in the Danger Room before handling solo missions. Inevitably you start to doubt yourself. How did I send this child out into the universe so ill prepared? How will they venture across time and space to combat super villains, when they don't even know which soap to use?

Not to worry, you've done your best. When the time comes, everything will click. Like Marvel's first family, the Richardses, from Nathaniel to Reed to Franklin,

STRANGE MESSAGES YOU MIGHT GET FROM YOUR ADULT CHILD:

- "How often do you wash bath towels?"
- "Is it bad if I alter the fabric of the universe?"
- "How many chicken nuggets do I usually order?"

COMMUNICATION POWER GRID – AGE 18 AND BEYOND		
Awareness:	▰▰▰▰▰▰▰▰▰	
Verbalization:	▰▰▰▰▰▰▰▰▰	
Comprehension:	▰▰▰▰▰▰▰▰▰	
Combativeness:	▰▰▱▱▱▱▱▱	

your children carry both your superhuman DNA and your legacy. Whether that's a burden or they thrive is up to them, but you've set them on the right path. Know you've done enough. You've raised a fully capable grown-up. And your kids will never stop needing you, and that's a good thing.

USING YOUR POWERS FOR GOOD

Ultimately as parents, we want our kids to thrive, survive, and find success. That's our end goal. You've had a hand in molding this human from day one, so it's natural to want to set high expectations. As we've discussed elsewhere in the book, encouragement while your child is finding themselves is key, but there's also a fine line between rallying and being overbearing. Your teen is trying to manage becoming their own independent self, but in most cases they are also striving to make you proud. This is a delicate balance that can be a lot

TIP Should your child exhibit signs of becoming Superior Iron Man once they leave the nest, call (212) 970-4133 and give them a good talking-to.

of pressure. Giving them guidance and courage along the way is the best way to show your support and help them on their own heroic journey.

When talking about managing the greatest of expectations between a parent and their child, there is no more perfect example than the father and son duo of Howard and Tony Stark. Howard Stark was incredibly successful and a prolific inventor. With that lineage, Tony had a lot to live up to, and the weight of that was sometimes hard for him to bear. Like all parents, Howard expected much of his son. There was an omnipresent assumption that young Tony would someday take the wheel of the Stark enterprise. But Tony was his own person, with his own interests and abilities. As it turned out, the creation of his Iron Man armor and taking on the persona of a protector allowed him to tap into all the good qualities he admired in his father, while still keeping his sense of self. The experience of living in a person's shadow is universal, and as the parent all you can do is reassure your child that if they stay the course, they will inevitably

find their own hero within—and one that may be even bigger and brighter than the one that leads the way.

Sometimes we as parents face great expectations just as much as our kids. Ramonda, the Queen Mother of Wakanda, had to lean on her morals and steadfast spiritual beliefs as lifelines for T'Challa and Shuri when they lost their father. She was expected to raise two children alone, be the matriarch of Wakanda, and prepare her kids to someday rule a nation. All eyes looked to her for the next steps and to make the tough decisions. With her spirituality as her guide, Ramonda's intelligence, leadership, and heart provided a foundation for her royal family. Her life lessons were absorbed

and emulated, giving T'Challa and Shuri the tools and the knowledge they needed to succeed. In the same way, you can advise your children the best you can, and hopefully they will use those lessons to make their path their own.

As a parent, always make sure that you're cheering on and encouraging while keeping your expectations in check. Preparing your child to embark on their own journey is scary, but you can only hope that the lessons you've given and the values you've instilled will be remembered when needed, and your child will figure out what works for them. If the path is similar to yours, you can help guide the way. If it's not, that's okay too. Time, patience, and a little self-discovery never hurt anyone. Unless they decide to become Superior Iron Man and reverse their morality and take a dark path...uh, maybe that's something for another book.

YOUR FUTURE CHILD

The unknown future is something some parents fear the most. Will your kids grow up to be heroes or villains? Will they harness the powers they were given for fighting for justice or will they decide to change the world with just one snap? It's not always that easy, because let's face it, sometimes those lines are blurred. And to be honest, sometimes what happens in one chronology is completely different from another. Meaning, if your child should go down the wrong path, there's still hope that things can change and all will be right in your timeline.

Nathan Summers, Cable, an Alpha Mutant with telepathic powers to cross dimensions, was infected with a deadly techno-organic virus as a baby. To save him, Nathan's father, Cyclops, took him to the thirty-eighth century of an alternate reality. Cable is from the future but his life is determined by his family's choices throughout time. Like Cable, your child is the living link between the past, present, and future. For kids going out on their own for the first time, the pressure of high standards and wanting to do right by your family can be difficult. Allowing them to figure things out on their own without always swooping in for a heroic save is a hard thing for a parent when your natural instinct is to protect. Sometimes you have to just let them body-slide through life like Cable does, and hope they figure it out on their own.

There will be times when your kid comes back to you with questions about your own past, because they want

to relate it to how that's shaping their own lives. These queries shouldn't be dismissed. While talking about the past can be difficult for some parents, it will help your child understand their own feelings and mistakes, and hopefully make their own future a little bit clearer. At this stage your child is nearing adulthood, yet it will feel like they're the same little toddler who was full of wonder and curiosity. Be prepared to answer your child in your own time, on your own terms, being as open as you are comfortable with.

The best thing you can do for your child is to set them up for the future you want them to have. Reed

Richards wanted a better tomorrow and saw that the way to achieve that is to put the future in the hands of those who will live it. By forming Future Foundation—a think tank of the most brilliant young minds in the universe—he tries to set the world on the right path by having the kids be the ones who make their own way. The same can be said for your own kids. By giving them the fundamentals of being a good person, making the right choices, and doing right by others, you set them up for success. Creating a mindset of being a good person sounds like such a simple thought, but at its core it's what will give your child the edge in being the best they can be. Show them the way. There's a fine line between heroes and villains but you need to allow them to become the leaders you know they're capable of being.

Whether traveling to different dimensions or moving to another state, your child will take what you've

SUGGESTED READING

Fantastic Four #1 (2012)—Reed Richards brought together the world's most brilliant young minds regardless of race, creed, color, gender, or species to create the Future Foundation, as a way of creating a hopeful, better tomorrow.

taught with them. All those years when you were sure that your child was ignoring you, you'll find that your impact is greater than you think. From little things like looking both ways crossing the street, to larger ideas like saving money for a rainy day, the lessons, the warnings, the long nights of training in the Danger Room—these are things they will carry with them for years. And you can rest easy that you set up your child's future with compassion, understanding, and intense battle preparedness.

THE DOOR (OR PORTAL) IS ALWAYS OPEN

Once free from school and ready for adulthood, some kids are ready to run. If you live in a small town they may be itching to move to the big city. Conversely, if you live in a metropolis they may be looking inward toward a quiet life they've never experienced. The first taste of freedom is a big one. For some it can be everything they dreamed of, but for others it may make them miss home and family even more.

Your children are an extension of you, and so providing a safe environment for them to come back with questions or ask for advice is how you know you've done a good job raising them. Whether it's to borrow something, ask about familial misunderstandings because of Skrull activity, or even just to say hello, any visit from your child is a welcome one. If they return a little worse for wear, try to be understanding. You don't know how many realities they've visited, or how many super villains they've defeated, and it doesn't matter. What matters is that you're there for them.

When Peter Parker is out fighting crime, he always comes home to Aunt May through his bedroom window. Leaving that line of communication open (metaphorically speaking) is the best way to show your child that you care. You want them to be able to return, wash their super suit, and tell you their recent otherworldly

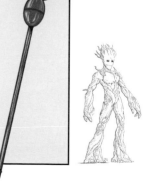

THINGS YOUR CHILD WILL ALWAYS RETURN HOME TO "BORROW":

1. Anything in your pantry. Your grocery run is their restock.

2. Staff of One. I mean, their blood unlocks it. Can you blame them?

3. Money. No explanation necessary, this ask will never end.

4. Vibranium. A little goes a long way.

5. Vehicle. Be it the family sedan or the Fantasti-Car out back, your car is better mostly because you have a full tank of gas.

PETER PARKER'S House

MIDTOWN HIGH SCHOOL 3 BLOCKS WEST

PETER'S ROOM

AS SPIDER-MAN, PETER SECRETLY ENTERS HOUSE THROUGH UPSTAIRS WINDOW.

PETER IS A WONDERFUL BOY! I JUST WISH HE WEREN'T SO FRAIL AND DELICATE!

LOCATED ON A QUIET STREET IN THE FOREST HILLS SECTION OF NEW YORK, IS THE NEAT FRAME, TWO-STORY HOUSE WHERE PETER LIVES WITH HIS DOTING, GENTLE AUNT MAY!

adventures and anything else they may want to talk about. Offering the option of a safe home base is the most rewarding part of parenting a super hero.

Open and honest communication is important when keeping that connection with your adult child. We all make mistakes and we all need advice, and keeping an open mind is probably the most uphill battle of later-years parenting. Understand that your baby is not a baby in the physical sense, and that they need to figure out life by living. Unless you're Groot, then there's always that possibility of regrowth.

That being said, your child will always be your baby in your heart, and your need to protect them is fierce... and can sometimes manifest into negative energy that may not be well received. Feeling judged as an adult child can evoke insecurity, and sometimes you have to just stand down, listen, and be understanding.

There will be times when they come to you with the most difficult life questions, and you may not always have the answers. But whether you keep your phone on, give them a key to the house, or use a Sling Ring to open a portal to their location, just channel your inner Aunt May when they pop through the window, and welcome them with open arms. They'll always know they can come back to you for advice, laughter, and love.

CONCLUSION

FOR NEARLY TWO DECADES NOW, you've nurtured a creature from a mushy pile of malleable goo into a strong and confident adult. Just as the Ancient One, Yao, had to trust that the teachings and wisdom he passed to generations of Sorcerer Supremes like Doctor Strange would endure before leaving our mortal plane, you too have to trust that you have prepared your child for the greatest challenges both expected and unexpected.

Treasure every nanosecond you experience on this journey. At the end of it you may find yourself overwhelmed, remembering first watching your newborn baby sleep, your toddler champion something they've struggled with, your tween when they began to blossom, your teenager making their own decisions, and your adult child take on the universe. As you relive those moments, your chest will start to swell, joyous

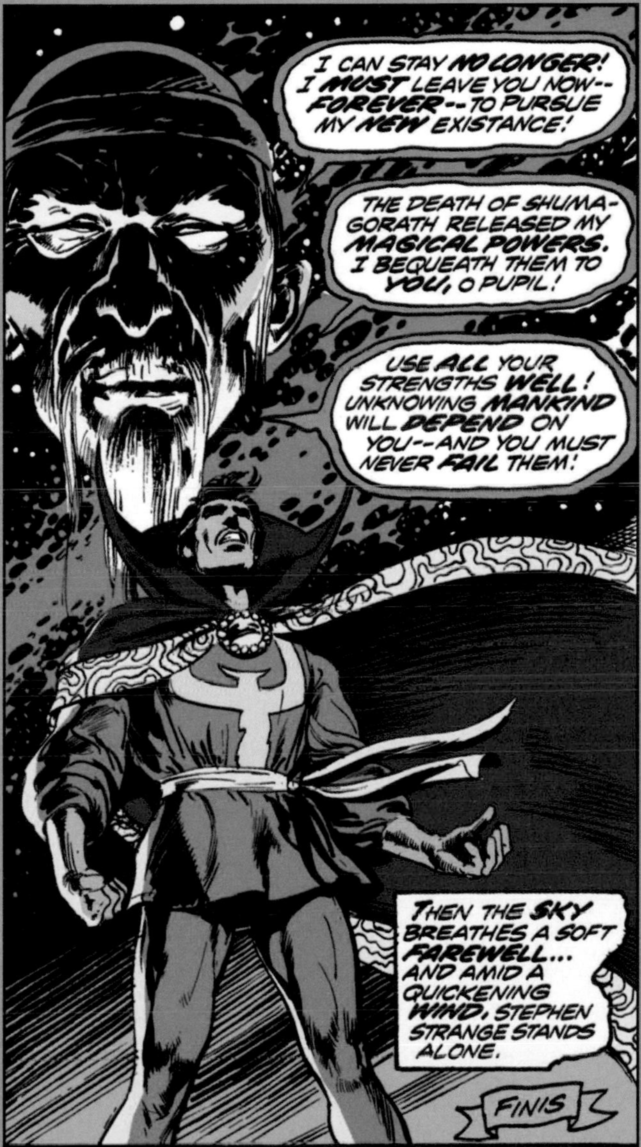

I CAN STAY NO LONGER! I MUST LEAVE YOU NOW-- FOREVER--TO PURSUE MY NEW EXISTANCE!
THE DEATH OF SHUMA-GORATH RELEASED MY MAGICAL POWERS. I BEQUEATH THEM TO YOU, O PUPIL!
USE ALL YOUR STRENGTHS WELL! UNKNOWING MANKIND WILL DEPEND ON YOU--AND YOU MUST NEVER FAIL THEM!
THEN THE SKY BREATHES A SOFT FAREWELL... AND AMID A QUICKENING WIND, STEPHEN STRANGE STANDS ALONE.
FINIS

endorphins will be released, and a tear may start building in your eye... Note: That reaction is not a mutant ability. It's not the result of exposure to radioactive radiation. It's not a sixth Spidey-Sense. It's not even a cosmic vision conjured by the Eye of Agamotto. That spark, that moment, that feeling—is parenting.

You've worked tirelessly. You've struggled. You've succeeded. There have been hurdles and roadblocks that not even Destiny could have seen coming. But we leave you with this one final thought: Even without en-

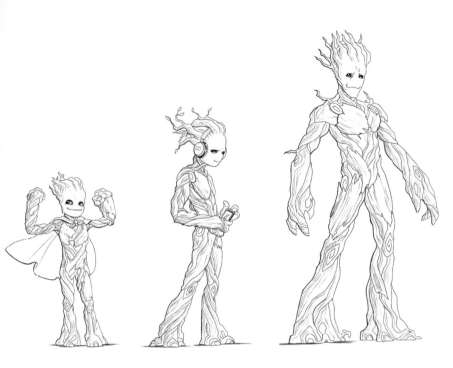

hanced abilities, just by being born your child is a time traveler. They will see the future. They will see a world that is completely foreign to you. You've instilled in them memories, lessons, strength, support, love, courage, and patience—and you've guided them through it all with a firm but tender hand. All of this sets the foundation for building their own future, and they will continue to hear your words of encouragement from beyond the astral plane. And that makes *you* the ultimate super hero.

ACKNOWLEDGMENTS

THANK YOU TO MY OWN PERSONAL FIRST FAMILY OF MARVEL, Alice Kawakami, Kyle, Tyler, and Mason Fujikawa, and Mark Kawakami. To the Defenders who always have my back and would do anything for my kids, Mel Caylo, Chrissy Dinh, and Sarah Kuhn. To the Avengers I can always call on, Cheryl deCarvalho, Chrys Hasegawa, Liza Palmer, Robb Pearlman, and Mary Yogi. To Lisa Arellano, Luz Rodriguez, Caroline Sanjume, Pam Swart, and Sara Webster, the ultimate team of super-moms who were always there to save the day. To Troy Benjamin, I'm always happy to be your co-author in the trenches of the Mojoverse. To our illustrator, Megan Levens, thank you for making our pages sparkle as bright as Dazzler. To the Watchers of our book universe at Marvel, Sven Larsen, Sarah Singer, Jeremy West, and Jeff Youngquist, your guidance has been much appreciated. To all the True Believers who are just trying to do their best parenting, you got this. —J.F.

IN ADDITION TO MY INCREDIBLE PARENTS, Jim and Isabell, I would like to thank the *true* strongest Avenger, Kelly, for being my sounding board for life and, as a result, this book. Thanks to my Personal Avenger Richard...who is out for a walk with the baby as I write this acknowledgment. Huge thanks to our resolute publishing team, Glenn, Leah, and Elizabeth, as well as the design team of Brigid, Monica, and Tara Long. And to my co-author, Jenn, for bringing me into this endeavor. Thanks for insisting I sleep at least forty-five minutes to write a few of these sections. But more so, thanks for preparing me to face the years I've yet to experience. Finally, a dedication to the late Stephen "Mr. O" Obrecht—who, despite having three kids, seven grandkids, and numerous foster kids, found the capacity to be a dad-away-from-dad for *at least* hundreds of us Franktown kids. I hear a lot of your guidance in what we've written here. You still owe me a root beer when I meet you in Valhalla. The good kind, not that generic stuff. —T.B.

ABOUT THE AUTHORS

JENN FUJIKAWA is a lifestyle and pop culture author, content creator, and host. She has created content for Lucasfilm, Marvel, Disney, Ghostbusters, and more. She is the author of multiple fandom-based cookbooks including *Star Wars: The Life Day Cookbook, Star Wars: The Padawan Cookbook, Avengers Campus: The Official Cookbook, Parks and Recreation: The Official Cookbook, The Princess Bride: The Official Cookbook,* and many, many, so many more. Born and raised in Los Angeles, if she's not writing, Jenn is cooking or asking her kids to take out the garbage. For more of Jenn's daily life, check out her Instagram @justjennrecipes.

TROY BENJAMIN is the Los Angeles–based author of *The Wakanda Files, Guidebook to the Marvel Cinematic Universe, How to Paint Characters the Marvel Studios Way*, and *Marvel's Agents of S.H.I.E.L.D. Declassified*. In addition to Marvel, he's also been fortunate to collaborate on the most beloved properties in popular culture including Star Wars, Ghostbusters, Transformers, Alien, X-Files, and more. Born in Colorado, Troy plays hockey, skis, and can't believe his wife is always cold in temperate Los Angeles. He spends every moment possible with his two kids, who tolerate their childlike father.

YOUR FAMILY HERE